SUMMA PUBLICATIONS, INC.

Thomas M. Hines
Publisher

Norris J. Lacy
Editor-in-Chief

Phillip Crant
Consulting Editor

Editorial Board

Benjamin F. Bart
University of Pittsburgh

William Berg
University of Wisconsin

Germaine Brée
Wake Forest University

Michael Cartwright
McGill University

Hugh M. Davidson
University of Virginia

John D. Erickson
Louisiana State University

Wallace Fowlie
Duke University (Retired)

James Hamilton
University of Cincinnati

Freeman G. Henry
University of South Carolina

Edouard Morot-Sir
*University of North Carolina
Chapel Hill*

Jerry C. Nash
University of New Orleans

Albert Sonnenfeld
Princeton University

Ronald W. Tobin
*University of California
Santa Barbara*

Philip A. Wadsworth
University of South Carolina (Retired)

ORDERS:
Box 20725
Birmingham, AL 35216

EDITORIAL ADDRESS:
1904 Countryside
Lawrence, KS 66044

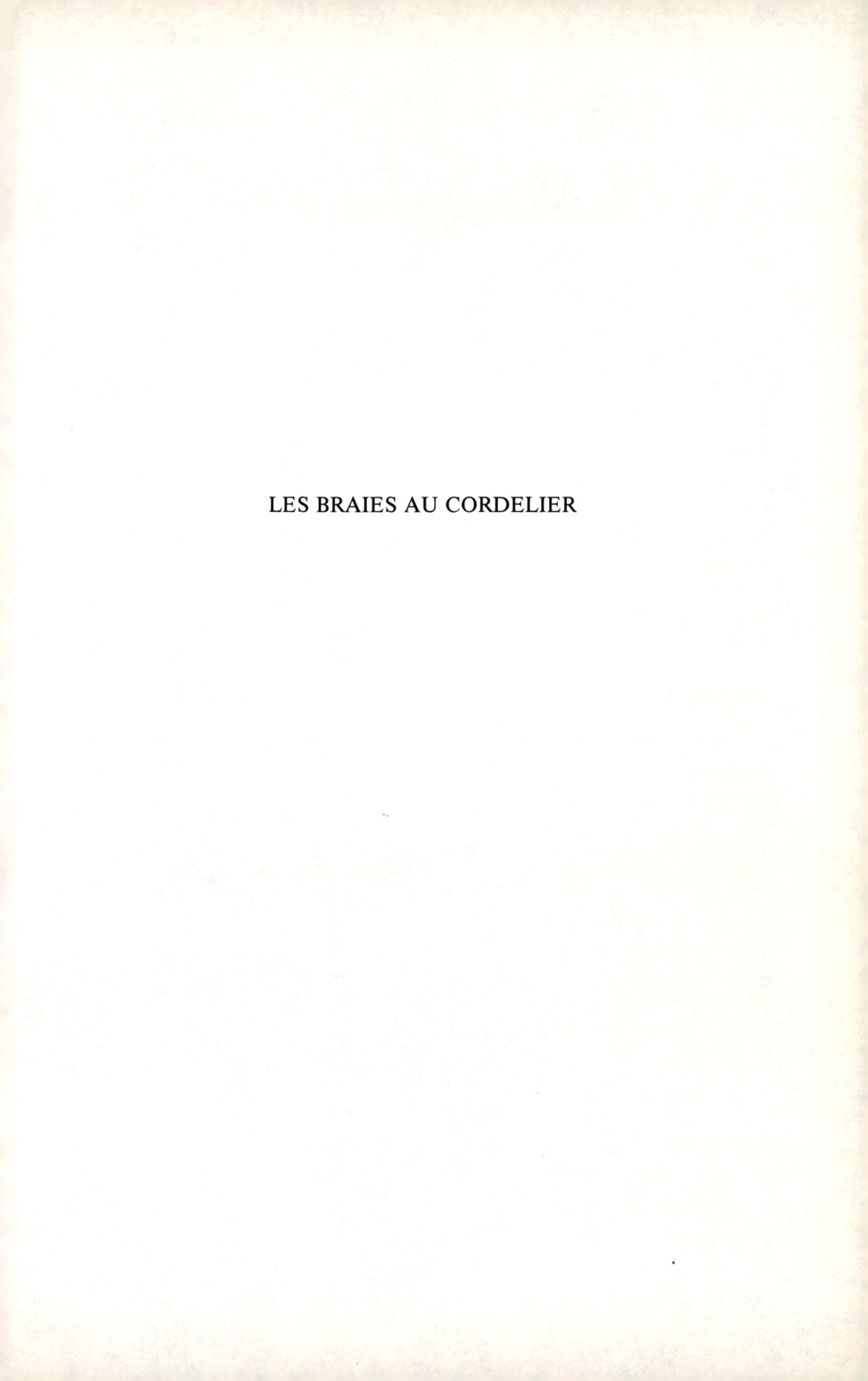

LES BRAIES AU CORDELIER

LES BRAIES AU CORDELIER

Anonymous Fabliau of the Thirteenth Century

A Critical Edition
With Introduction, Notes, and Glossary

In Appendix
Les Braies le Prestre by Jean de Condé
La Farce de Frere Guillebert
And Other French Analogues

Edited by
Richard O'Gorman

SUMMA PUBLICATIONS, INC.
Birmingham, AL
1983

Copyright 1983
Summa Publications, Inc.
ISBN 0-917786-35-1
Library of Congress Catalog Card Number 83-50519
Printed in the United States of America

Toute femme doit en personne
S'en acquitter trois fois le mois
Vers les enfants de saint François;
Cela fondé sur l'Ecriture.

La Fontaine

PREFACE

In the course of my reading of the Old French fabliaux prior to choosing a number of texts for a collection of translations, I selected for inclusion as representative of the genre *Les Braies au cordelier*. But practical considerations led to its elimination from the collection in favor of its analogue, *Les Braies le prestre* by Jean de Condé. Numerous rereadings of the text however served only to confirm my initial admiration for its tight narrative structure, its humorously malicious tone, and especially its elements of verbal parody which, in my opinion, make it a masterpiece of the fabliau genre. It became increasingly apparent that a modern critical edition was needed to replace the outdated text of Montaiglon-Raynaud—an edition devoid of commentary, based on the less desirable manuscript, and possessing those shortcomings we have come to associate with the *Recueil général*.

The typescript was kindly read by two former students, Rosalie Vermette and Norris Lacy, to whom I owe the elimination of numerous blunders and errors. I am also indebted to Arnold Perkins and Jane Eckhardt who did much of the tedious checking in the latter stages of composition. I should like to acknowledge their generous assistance, reserving for myself responsibility for any deficiencies which may yet remain in my work. I owe a special debt of gratitude to Professor William Roach, whose initial instruction in the study of Old French texts was invaluable and whose help and encouragement over the years have been given unstintingly. It is a pleasure for me to acknowledge it here. Finally, my sincere thanks are offered to the Graduate College of the University of Iowa for the generous financial contribution towards the publication of this work.

West Branch, Iowa   R. O'G.
March, 1982

CONTENTS

- I. Preface iii
- II. Introduction 1
  1. Manuscripts 1
  2. Previous Editions 2
  3. Date 3
  4. Composition and Style 5
  5. Language and Versification 16
     a. Table of Rhymes 16
     b. Versification 22
     c. Language of the Author 23
     d. Language of the Scribe 27
- III. Text 30
- IV. Notes 43
- V. Index of Proper Names 57
- VI. Glossary 59
- VII. Appendices: Analogues 75
  1. *Les Braies le prestre* by Jean de Condé 76
  2. *Le Livre du chevalier de la Tour Landry* 83
  3. *La Farce de Frere Guillebert* 85
  4. *Apologie pour Hérodote* by Henri Estienne 119
  5. *La Culotte des cordeliers* by Le Grand d'Aussy 121
- VIII. Bibliography and Abbreviations 127

Richard O'Gorman

INTRODUCTION

1. *Manuscripts*

Les Braies au cordelier is extant in two manuscripts of the last quarter of the thirteenth century, both preserved in the Bibliothèque Nationale: *fonds français* 837, folios 154c-156b (siglum *A*), and 19152, folios 120f-122b (siglum *D*). Because of the large number of previously published works they contain, these codices are too well known to medievalists to warrant description here. They have both been published in complete facsimile editions: Henri Omont, *Fabliaux, dits et contes en vers français du XIIIe siècle: Fac-similè du manuscrit français 837 de la Bibliothèque Nationale* (Paris, 1932), and Edmond Faral, *Le manuscrit 19152 du fonds français de la Bibliothèque Nationale* (Paris, 1934).

As in the case of most two-manuscript traditions the choice of a base manuscript is not easy. An examination of the textual variants reveals that both are acceptable copies of the fabliau, provided that we take into account the usual number of scribal slips, blunders, and personal innovations occasioned by the precarious nature of manuscript transmission.[1] And they are close enough to one another in the text they transmit that it is tempting to argue that, if not actually copied from the same model, very few intermediaries must have intervened between these two witnesses and their archetype. Where they do differ, in the great majority of divergent readings both are intelligible and for the most part correct in meter and rhyme. However, certain features of *D* serve to make it the better witness to the tradition:

1) Mistakes in *A*: *amast* (20), *dun* (20), *icel* (128), *chacier* (241), *estovra* (356), *autres* (225).

2) Inferior readings in *A*: *en bon point* (46), *dolor* (83), *sus* (86), *fu farouche* (130, see n. 126), *fu geun* (265), *sen vint* (284), *Dites moi fet il bone dame* (286), *Vous savez* (287), *dune part* (324).

3) Ms *D* contains three couplets not in *A* (279-80, 299-300, 315-16). It is for all practical purposes impossible to determine whether *D*

---

[1]"Variantes peu nombreuses et peu importantes" (Rychner, I, 32).

interpolated these couplets or whether *A* deleted them since in no case is the information essential to the narrative. In all three cases however the *D* text does seem superior.

4) In vs 2, we should doubtless consider the *A* reading an innovation since the designation of the work as a *dit* would contradict *flabel* found in the last verse, and which, this time, is in agreement with *D*.

5) Finally, vss 5-6 are markedly inferior in *A* where the appeal to both an oral and a written source is suspicious. Ms *D*, in a typical literary appeal to the truth of the subject of the tale, presents the couplet in a far more logical way since the narrative follows directly on *Il avint*.

But *D* is not without its faults, as numerous emendations and some corrections were deemed necessary. To be sure, most of these—all taken from *A*—are very minor, and many are of a purely mechanical nature: a *bourdon* entailed the loss of vs 40; thoughtless repetitions of words at the beginning of verses at 46, 125, 326; mechanical slips like *se mist* for *s'en ist* (66), *commande a* for *commanda a* (195), *jorz* for *torz* (239), etc.; hypometric verses easily rectified at 90, 195, 273; fall of *s* in *un clers* (7) and *Lor* (111). Others are more serious: *Que* for *Quant* (73) destroys the syntactical construction *Quant. . .Lors; repairiez* at vs 110 violates the rhyme. Since the author does adhere closely to the two-case system, I have corrected *voisins* (154). On the whole however the text of *D* preserves more verses and poses fewer editorial problems than *A*, and it has thus been adopted as the base manuscript for the edition of *Les Braies au cordelier*.

In the treatment of the text I follow generally accepted practices among editors of Old French literature. All corrections and emendations are taken from *A* and the rejected readings noted at the foot of the page. Complete variant readings from *A* are listed beneath the rejected readings. Contractions and abbreviations are solved in accordance with the scribal forms when written in full. Roman numerals have been written out, and the consonantal value of *v* and *j* has been distinguished from vocalic *u* and *i*. Paragraph indentations are my own.

2. *Previous Editions*

There are three previous published editions of *Les Braies au cordelier:*

E. Barbazan, *Fabliaux et contes des poëtes françois des XII, XIII,*

XIV, et XVes siècles, tirés des meilleurs auteurs, 3 vols. (Paris-Amsterdam, 1756). II, 14-32.

M. Méon, *Fabliaux et contes des poëtes françois des XI, XII, XIII, XIV, et XVe siècles, tirés des meilleurs auteurs, publiés par Barbazan: Nouvelle édition augmentée et revue sur les manuscrits de la Bibliothèque Impériale*, 4 vols. (Paris, 1808). III, 169-180.

Anatole de Montaiglon et Gaston Raynaud, *Recueil général et complet des fabliaux des XIIIe et XIVe siècles*, 6 vols. (Paris, 1872-1890). III, 275-287.

The *Braies* was one of the first Old French texts brought to light in the eighteenth century by Barbazan, and it became the object of an adaptation into Modern French prose some twenty years later by Le Grand d'Aussy, *Fabliaux ou contes du XIIe et du XIIIe siècle*, 3 vols. (Paris, 1779), II, 66-73, under the title *La Culotte des cordeliers* (printed in Appendix 5). In all three cases the editors based the text on ms *A*, and in the *Recueil général* the editors provided variants from *D* and incorporated some emendations, notably the three couplets missing in *A*. While these editions are not without value today, they do not measure up to modern standards of textual criticism. In addition, in my view they were based on the wrong manuscript, they are presented without commentary, and finally (and least important of course) they are all difficult to find in any but the well-stocked research library. I am hopeful that the present edition will fill a need in the study of the Old French fabliau.

3. *Date*

As in the case of the great majority of fabliaux, a date of composition for *Les Braies au cordelier* cannot be determined with any degree of accuracy. We can however get an idea of the period of composition by considering evidence adduced from the narrative itself. We shall see that the most likely time frame falls between the end of the second and the beginning of the third quarter of the thirteenth century, that is during the second generation of fabliau authors (assuming that Jean Bodel was the earliest author of fabliaux) when the techniques of the new literary form had fully evolved.

The mention of the Franciscan convent in Orleans at vss 242 ff as the place where the wife sought "to cover her shame" provides a real clue to the period of composition. The coming of the Franciscans to France dates from 1217 when they were established at Saint Denis; subsequently, perhaps as early as 1223, they expanded their foothold inside the city to the Montagne Sainte-Geneviève. Under the provincial Gregory of Naples (1223-1233), the order spread rapidly in Paris and establishments radiated throughout Northern France. The necrology of William of Barres (1233) names twenty-one convents of Minorite friars extending in a wide circle around Paris, and among them one at Orleans.[2] It is safe to assume then that a Franciscan house was established in the place of composition of the *Braies* ca. 1230, a rather firm *terminus a quo* for the work.[3] That the order was already considered so dissolute that the mere presence of the breeches of one of its members was deemed sufficient to promote conception[4] would argue for a date somewhat later in the century, a period roughly contemporary with the writings of Rutebeuf.[5] His fabliau *Frere Denise* (Bastin-Faral, II, 283-291) also embodies an attack on the order of Minorites similar to that implicit in the *Braies*: an hypocritical friar entices a devout maiden to enter his order disguised as a boy in order to debauch her. Rutebeuf's manifest feelings of hostility towards the friar are, to be sure, more acerbic than those found in the *Braies,* but the satiric intent of both is clear: *cucullus non facit monachum.*

---

[2]Léopold Delisle, *Les rouleaux des morts du IX au XV siècles* (Paris, 1896), pp. 407-20. See also P. Gratien, *Histoire de la fondation et de l'évolution de l'Ordre des Frères Mineurs aux XIIIe* (Paris-Gembloux, 1928), p. 516, n. 6.

[3]Bastin-Faral, I, 65-68, and Placid Hermann, *XIIIth Century Chronicles* (with Introduction and Notes by Marie-Thérèse Laureilhe) (Chicago, 1961), pp. 210-13.

[4]In the words of Henry C. Lea, *The History of Sacerdotal Celibacy in the Christian Church* (New York, 1957): "The exaggerated purity and mortification of the early followers of the blessed St. Francis had long since yielded to the temptations which attended on the magnificent success of the institution, and the mystic aspirations which earned for it the name of the Seraphic Order degenerated into sloth and crime which took advantage of the opportunities afforded by the privilege to hear confessions" (p. 298).

[5]Note that the first attestation of *cordelier* recorded by the *T.-L.,* II, 854, is from Rutebeuf's poems on the mendicant orders.

Seen in the context of the mendicant orders, certain vocabulary associated with the friar would seem to take on a deeper meaning. Upon approaching him, the wife *li regehi* (243) her dilemma, and later the merchant seeks out the friar *qui devoit deslïer La borgoise* (320). The verb *regehir*, while possible in the sense of 'to relate,' was most often employed with a religious meaning 'to confess,' and *deslïer* implied 'to absolve of one's sins' (see n. 320). If we hear an echo of confessional vocabulary here, as I think we must, the implication would then be that the Franciscan priests had acquired the power of the confessional by the time of the composition of the *Braies*. This power was granted in 1237 by Gregory IX in the bull *Quoniam abundavit iniquitas* (Bastin-Faral, I, 67), in spite of the injunction of Lateran IV against the preaching orders' attempts to usurp the prerogatives of the parish priest. In the context of the struggle which ensued the author may well have intended, in the figure of the Franciscan, a humorous rebuke against the pretentions of the mendicants to encroach upon the power of absolution of the secular clergy.

There is some evidence then, albeit circumstantial, for placing the composition of *Les Braies au cordelier* in the period 1240-1260, contemporary *grosso modo* with Rutebeuf with whom the author shared a real contempt for the Minorites, with Henri d'Andeli and the authors of the *Roman de la Rose* with whom he shared many of the same dialectal features and even the same geographical provenance (see Language of the Author, p. 27). This period would also be consistent with the author's handling of the couplet, his conscious preference for rich and leonine rhymes, and his use of homonymic and equivocal rhyme (see Versification, p. 22-23).

4. *Composition and Style*

Although we need not concern ourselves with the ongoing debate regarding the definition of the fabliau, a cursory reading of *Les Braies au cordelier* is sufficient to proclaim it a "classic" of the genre. Not only does the author clearly label his work a *flabel* (360), what Dubuis has termed a "fabliau certifié," but in subject matter, characters, form, and style it rivals the very best of the fabliaux.

In the choice of the subject the *Braies* belongs to the largest category studied by Nykrog (p. 55), the "thème érotique." In the first of Nykrog's subdivisions it falls into the "triangulaire" group (63 fabliaux), then into the subgroup whose issue is "favorable aux amants" (24). The final division into two categories, "mari malmené" (11) and "mari contenté (13), is a distinction which does not apply to the *Braies* for, although the hapless merchant is not physically abused (as he is in the *Bourgeoise d'Orléans*), he is dishonored, humiliated and made the object of ridicule by his companions. Nykrog finds this theme of the erotic triangle with favorable outcome for the woman (husband duped) not only the largest in number but representative of the earliest examples of the genre: the three tales specifically designated "fabliau" in the translation of the *Disciplina clericalis* and the two triangle tales from the *Ysopets* of Marie de France.[6]

The *dramatis personae* of the *Braies* are, characteristically, unnamed. They are the stock characters of so many of the fabliaux: the wife, her merchant husband, and a clerk, with secondary roles given to the merchant's companion and to a Franciscan friar who is but a device introduced to tie together the threads of the narrative at the dénouement.

The wife is described in the most unflattering of terms. She possesses most of the traits, or rather vices, of the wife of the typical erotic fabliau. She is adulterous and totally unscrupulous in her pursuit of the pleasures of the flesh. In her there is no psychological malaise, no qualms of conscience, and above all no hesitation in her infidelity. The author describes her infatuation in the most matter-of-fact terms: it is not the clerk she loves, but *du clerc le solaz* (20), merely to lie naked with him in bed. She is bold in receiving her lover minutes after she sends her husband out the door, confident that she can cover any unforeseen mishap. And her cunning does not fail her when not one but two contretemps ensue. Her overly dramatic protestations of love for her husband upon his unexpected return deftly serve to allay his fears, but the quickly devised strategem to explain the presence of the clerc's breeches in the bed is truly wondrous. And to add insult to injury her narrow escape leaves her unrepentant. In short, she possesses those qualities condemned in all the codes of *courtoisie*.

But the success of the wife's deceit depends directly on the obtuseness of the husband. Probably older, clearly affectionate towards his wife, he is no match for her *guenges et tors* (12). He is industrious in the pursuit of his livelihood but, in the wife's eyes, boorish to the point of exasperation and unmitigatingly gullible, a dupe to feminine wiles and clerical unscrupulous-

---

[6]For an analysis of the erotic fabliaux "à triangle" inspired by the narratological model of Greimas, see Michel Olsen, *Les Transformations du triangle érotique* (Copenhague, 1976), pp. 61-72.

ness. Totally persuaded in the end of his wife's faithfulness, he swears never to doubt her again. What a delight this portrait must have been for an audience scornful of the merchant class.

The clerk's character is less delineated. He is presented as a foil in the action, a stereotypical figure of uxorious seduction common to the fabliaux. Eager to do the wife's bidding, he readily accepts her money, and, if not particularly troubled by the straits he finds himself in, he quickly goes along with her attempts to extricate herself. These *clerici ribaldi*, the *clercs écoliers* of so many fabliaux, are always victorious in their amorous exploits and always triumph over their rivals, usually the husbands of their paramours, regardless of their social station. This observation led Nykrog (p. 132) to speculate that the authors of a great many of the fabliaux must have come from this class of wandering students, the *vagantes* responsible for so many of the humorous tales and so much of the satiric verse of the period.[7]

These three characters are presented without malice and certainly without satiric intent. The same cannot be said for the Franciscan. Although he is not directly implicated in the sexual tryst, he does assume willingly the conspiratorial role in the wife's plan to exonerate herself. Not that the fabliaux do not offer an abundance of unworthy and unscrupulous clerics, but rarely is a specific order of clerics indicted. And the author insists by twice naming him a *cordelier* (314, 319), and three times designating him by the more familiar *frere menor* (242, 257) or *frere menuz* (339) for good measure. To my mind, this insistence betrays a clear intent to denigrate a religious order whose original aspirations had already been subverted. Like Rutebeuf,[8] he implies that the members of the Minorite order had strayed from the purpose envisaged by Saint Francis and had become in a very short time an order of worldly monks of tainted morality. Let it be noted however that the satire directed as it is against an individual or a group of clerics is not an attack on the powers of the clergy as such—although the priest was fair game, his office was not.

---

[7] See Stephen L. Wailes, "*Vagantes* and the Fabliaux," in Cooke-Honeycutt, pp. 43-58.

[8] Initially approving the Franciscans (see *Le dit des cordeliers*, Bastin-Faral, I, 231-41), once in Paris Rutebeuf bitterly opposed the Mendicants, including the Minorites, in a poem *Les ordres de Paris*

The structure of the narrative is most carefully worked out. In typical fashion the author presents his tale as the truth, *par verité* (4). But he goes even further: he cites as his source someone who bears witness to this truth (4-5), and he affirms that it happened as he heard it (6). This appeal to veracity is reinforced in the course of the narrative by alleging eyewitnesses at the fair in Meung: *Si con tesmoignent mainte gent* (272) and *Ce me reconurent Aucun qui en la place furent* (279-80). Such insistence on the authenticity of the facts of the story is, according to Dubuis (pp. 143 ff), one of the most persistent, even predictable features of a true fabliau. But the author of the *Braies* contradicts one of Dubuis' conclusions regarding this appeal: "Les auteurs, dans leur ensemble, en sont restés à l'affirmation gratuite de l'authenticité des faits, et n'ont pas tenté de la renforcer. . .par des allusions précises ou des détails évocateurs" (p. 152). As we have seen, the author does indeed reinforce his appeal to the truth, and in situating the action in Orleans he places the fair realistically at Meung, a convenient distance from the city for a morning's journey. Furthermore, the reference to the Franciscans at Orleans, and even perhaps the oath on *seinte Croiz* (170), reinforces this localization. Contrary to Dubuis' assertion then, Orleans simply could not be changed to Poitiers or Soissons without the necessity of making other changes in the text. In short, the localization, which stresses the author's claim to truth, was not injected "après coup et comme au hasard" (p. 147).

This does not mean of course that we should reject Dubuis' conclusion that this is a purely conventional appeal to truth, little more than a formality, a "game" employed by storytellers of all ages. Indeed, it could be argued that such an insistence on the "truth" of what will turn out to be a humorously improbable (and in some fabliaux impossible) story amounts to that sort of discrepancy which contributes to the comic effect of the tale. By its very nature such an appeal instantly alerts the audience to the fact that a fabliau is to follow, and we easily imagine a smile creeping across the

---

(Bastin-Faral, I, 323-39). The dissolute life led by the Friars prompted Rutebeuf to lament in the *Dit de Sainte Eglise* (Bastin-Faral, I, 279-85):

> Quant cil qui jurent es palliz
> Nous font orandroit grant moleste
> S'il n'ont bons vins et les blanz liz.
> Se Diex les a pour ce esliz,
> Pour po perdi sainz Poz la teste.

118

face of a listener at the mere mention of *voir* or *verité*. But in the case of the *Braies*, the author reinforced his original claim in the course of the narrative, and he did make the effort to provide it with a plausibly realistic setting.

Few fabliaux exemplify better than *Les Braies au cordelier* Nykrog's thesis that these rhymed tales actually represent "des burlesques courtois."[9] Elements of verbal parody run throughout the text and have one purpose: to produce laughter by establishing a discrepancy between commonplace situations of adultery and casual fornication and the rhetorical style of refined love. Indeed, all through the tale there reverberates the language of *fin' amor*, language traditionally reserved for the high style. The key to this added humorous dimension to the work lies in the clash of the sublime style with characters of common extraction and situations unworthy of the great literature of courtly inspiration, a social level and behavior which clearly calls for the *stylus humilis* (Faral, pp. 86-89). By playing off the *gravis stylus* against unsuitable characters, settings, and actions, this continual interference between the stylistic registers produces a subtle but overt parodic humor which only a literarily sophisticated audience could grasp.[10] Rather than a work destined for the town or market place, the *Braies* surely demanded a courtly or learned milieu to be appreciated fully. Not that the bourgeois was incapable of understanding the implications of *courtoisie* or its parodic dimension in the fabliau, it was very likely irrelevant to him.[11]

---

[9] Nykrog, p. 71. See the summary of his arguments in "Courtliness and the Townspeople: The Fabliaux as a Courtly Burlesque" in Cooke-Honeycutt, pp. 59-73. My understanding of the referential nature of parody is put succinctly by J. Gerald Kennedy, "Parody as Exorcism: 'The Raven' and 'The Jewbird'," *Genre* 13 (1980), 161-69: "Unlike other literary modes, parody describes not an intrinsic structure or quality in a work but rather a condition of relationship to another text or set of texts. Parody creates a theoretical juxtaposition in which the more recent work ironically represents selected elements of its antecedent, usually through mocking exaggeration. . . .parody typically places in tension two authorial perspectives" (p. 161).

[10] See the excellent article by Saul N. Brody, "The Comic Rejection of Courtly Love," in Joan M. Ferrante and George D. Economou, *In Pursuit of Perfection: Courtly Love in Medieval Literature* (New York, 1975), pp. 221-61.

The echo of courtly expression is perhaps found at the very outset: *Mestre vueil m'entente et ma cure* (1), a commonplace expression of the *exordium* found widely in romance. The *Lai de Desiré* (ed. Tobin, pp. 169-205) begins:

> Entente i metrai et ma cure
> A rencunter une aventure[12] 2

This is followed by what is doubtless an allusion to the process of composition: the subject matter (*matire* 5) is given orally to the author (6) from which he fashions the story (*aventure* 2) which, in its elaboration, becomes a *flabel* (360). All this might well be reminiscent of Chrétien's application of *san* to the *matiere* given him in the *Lancelot* to produce a *molt bele conjointure* (*Erec* 12) which yields the romance, or the *mateire* (1) which Marie de France drew upon to relate the *aventure* (24) of *Guigemar*.

Once the parodic tone is established, the author, as did Henry d'Andeli in the *Lai d'Aristote*, eschews carefully all vulgarity or obscenity of expression. Like the authors of romance he never utters a vulgar word, never stoops to the level of crudeness so prevalent in many of the fabliaux.[13] His description of the wife and clerk's lovemaking is candid enough (79-88), but the act is described euphemistically as a *gieu* (214); the clerk is

---

[11] This disjunction between the form of a literary work and its content has been studied by Joseph A. Dane, "Parody and Satire: A Theoretical Model," *Genre* 13 (1980), 145-59. The author argues that his model of a parodic work would suppose that "readers can be legitimately expected to possess the necessary knowledge to interpret 'correctly' the author's intentions" (p. 154).

[12] See, among numerous examples, the *Meraugis de Portlesguez* (ed. Friedwagner): *Qui de rimoier s'entremet Et son cuer et s'entente i met* (2): the *Perceval* of Chrétien de Troyes: *Chrestiens, qui entente et paine. . .A rimoier* (66); the *Lancelot: que gueres n'i met fors sa painne et s'antancion* (29). Some fabliaux also employ the same rhetorical introduction in the *exordium: Ma paine metrai et m'entente* from *De .iii. dames qui troverent .i. vit* (*MR*, V, 32).

[13] While it is true that the word *putain* appears twice (156, 278) and *bordel* once (155), both are spoken in dialogue (or indirect discourse) and

acolez et baisiez (75), the wife *La bouche li baise* (212), and they *s'entrebaisent* (236) in imitation of the knights and ladies of romance. And like the lovers Perceval and Blancheflor in Chrétien's *Perceval*, the couple *Braz a braz jurent en la couche* (86).[14]

If this reminiscence of the *Perceval* seems farfetched, another so-called antiquote surely is not. The wife of the *Braies* watches over her husband, eager to wake him so that she can receive her lover: *Il dormi et ele veilla* (49). In Chrétien's *Erec et Enide* the faithful wife also watches over the sleeping Erec:

> Cil dormi, et cele veilla,
> Onques la nuit ne someilla   3049

There is no doubt in my mind that this is a direct parodic borrowing from a courtly situation: intelligible enough in itself, it gains measurably in its subtle echo of the courtly Enide.[15]

Patterns of courtly vocabulary are interwoven throughout the text in imitation of the elegant romance or *chanson d'amour*. The wife is *saige et cortoise* (8) she yearns for the clerc's *solaz* (20) and *delit* (24), she feigns that no man will have *soulaz ne delit* (140) from her save her husband. The author describes her lustful passion in the purest of courtly metaphors:

---

are appropriate to the characters' speech. Beyer, p. 101, distinguishes two types of fabliau, those which employ "direkte Obszönität" and those of "indirekte Obszönität," the obscenity of the first being aggressive and the second veiled and suggestive. The *Braies* clearly belongs to the second category which uses *courteises paroles* while avoiding *laiz* or *vilains motz* (the expressions are from Jean de Meung). See Beyer's chapter "Techniken der Glossierung durch *quelque courteise parole*," pp. 104-11.

[14]Despite the subtle arguments regarding the virginity of Perceval, *braz a braz* in both texts is nothing more than a polite euphemism for sexual intercourse. This expression was common in Old French (see the *T.-L.*, I, 1129), and most often it implied exactly what it does in the *Braies*. If not a specific echo from the *Perceval*, the expression *Braz a braz* in *Les Braies au cordelier* does at least draw on the euphemistic cliché of romance.

[15]In the words of Rychner: "Rapprocher, grâce à cette allusion, la

Comme cele qu'Amors ot mise Et bien enlaciee en ses laz (18-19),[16] a blasphemy against the god of love. The dialogue is sprinkled liberally with polite address which recalls the speech of courtly personages: the wife addresses her husband as *beau sire* (51 etc.), and he responds in the most refined terms, using up an entire verse: *Bele tres douce chiere amie* (145).[16a] The clerc calls the wife *Bele amie* (204), to which she responds *Beax amis* (210) and *Beax douz amis* (113).[17]

Two particularly revealing expressions stand out as ludicrous distortions of courtly situations, and they leave no doubt as to the parodic intention of the author. In describing the wife he proclaims:

> qui velt amer par amors
> Couvient savoir guenges et tors   12

Later she beseeches the clerc *Par amors* (227) to reveal what is on his belt. *Par amors* (and the *s* is assured by the rhyme) is the key expression applied by authors of romance to the refined love conceived according to the courtly code. It has been studied in detail by Jean Frappier (see n. 11) as it applies to the literature of courtly expression, and by Nykrog as one of the most significant elements of the courtly burlesque found in many of the fabliaux. The incongruity in its most economical form is exemplified by the verse *Amer par amours fame a çavatier* from the *Prestre qui fu mis au lardier* (Nykrog, p. 74), doubtless the same personage Marie de France described as *li vilain curteis* in the prologue to *Guigemar*. The same incongruity is blatant here, for there is nothing more diametrically opposed than the love

---

bourgeoise qui brûle d'accueillir son ami d'Enide la fidèle veillant sur le sommeil d'Erec!" (I, 35).

[16]The same courtly metaphor in the fabliau *Du clerc qui fu repus deriere l'escrin* by Jean de Condé (*MR*, IV, 47-52):

> En Haynau ot une bourgoise,
> En une ville, assez courtoise,   8
> Plaine de jeu et de soulas,
> K'amours le tenoit en ses las.

[16a]Cf. *Le Lai de l'Ombre* (ed. J. Orr): 'Bele tresdouce amie chiere,' *Fet il*, (350).

[17]Words such as *honor* and *honte* may also have had an aristocratic ring to them. They represent key notions in heroic and courtly literature

designated by the expression *amer par amors* and the necessity of possessing a knowledge of tricks and deceit in love to trick one's husband in order to slake a lustful passion.

One of the well-known injunctions for the courtly lover concerns the requirement of secrecy in love. In the words of Lazar, "La première règle de l'amour courtois est la discrétion absolue" (p. 177). Although Lanval escapes the disaster predicted if he disclosed the name of his ladylove, in one of the most successful of thirteenth-century *nouvelles*, the *Châtelaine de Vergi*, the action turns about the tragic results which befall the lovers when the knight failed to heed the injunction to secrecy. This precept was firmly imbedded in the codes of courtesy of the times. Drouart la Vache writes in his *Livre d'amours*, an adaption of the *De amore:*

> Se li dui amant sont saige,
> Bien celeront en lor coraige   658
> L'amour. . .
> Sachiez qu'Amours ne dure mie
> Longuement, puis qu'elle est seüe
> Et de la gent aperceüe   6524

But when the clerk utters the formula in its perfectly correct form, *Qui aime il doit s'amor celer* (206), the travesty of the courtly situation is blatantly cynical. We are far from the lofty situation of the *Châtelaine* where the disclosure of the secret love triggers jealous rage, death, suicide, and murder, all elements of high tragedy. Here we find a sordid affair of purely lustful dimensions: the clerk's concern is that the neighbors might see him leave the house. Surely such humor was not lost on an aristocratic audience familiar with the precepts of Andreas Capellanus.

It is clear then that the persistence of this expression of noble inspiration, inappropriate to the characters or to the situation, does not reveal merely isolated examples of parodic intent on the part of the author; rather, the text is so laden with courtly expressions and overtones that the work as a whole must be viewed as a deliberate parody of courtly literature.

An essential criterion for a successful comic tale is brevity of

---

whose meaning is difficult to define precisely (Burgess, p. 88), but they are often paired in romance literature: *Onor aveir, eschiver honte (Troie,* 8761). When the author foretells the husband's impending *desennor* (196), narration, all parts carefully ordered to bring about quickly the punch lines and in a sequence designed to produce laughter at the appropriate moment.[18] The author of the *Braies* was a master of the terse style. Such economy of narrative detail precludes *a priori* a leisurely treatment of the subject matter, character development, or peripheral excursions away from the single focus of the tale, the so-called *amplificatio* of rhetorical doctrine. This does not mean however that the author does not intervene from time to time in his narrative, but his intrusions are brief and have for specific purpose the establishment of a connivance between himself and his audience. He introduces the wife and comments on her deceit and lustful nature (9-24), or he exclaims at the inopportune return of the husband: *Diex! con ci a male nouvele!* (112). On occasion he makes ironic comments on what will happen: the merchant *ne set pas la desennor... Que li est cel jor avenue* (196-98), or *Par tans orra autres noveles Que ne li seront pas molt beles* (315-16). These momentary asides set up a sort of conspiracy with the audience which contributes to the comic effect and imposes a necessary distance between the audience and the story.[19]

One device employed by authors of fabliaux to promote narrative economy is the liberal use of direct discourse. A full one-third of the verses of the *Braies* contain dialogue. This narrative technique serves to characterize the personages, to enliven the tale with examples of realistic speech while at the same time moving the story rapidly towards its climax.

---

or refers to the wife's *honte* (15, 321) or to her attempt to explain the clerk's breeches in her bed *Por changier sa honte a hennor* (241), a court audience must surely have found cause for laughter at such noble words used in a context so basely inappropriate.

[18] On the importance of the preparation for the comic climax in generating the humor in these tales, see the study by Thomas D. Cooke, *The Old French and Chaucerian Fabliaux* (Columbia, Missouri, 1978).

[19] See Norris J. Lacy, "Types of Esthetic Distance in the Fabliaux," in Cooke-Honeycutt, pp. 107-117: "The result of this technique, whereby the author divulges the conclusion before developing the story, is the creation of a kind of dramatic irony. In a work that requires economy, this device is frequently the most efficient means of making the audience privileged observers of the action" (p. 117).

Another type of authorial intrusion also serves to accelerate the movement of events: on three occasions the author injects formulas of abridgement of the type *Que vos feroie demoree*? (44, see also 78, 281), clichés widely used in the fabliaux and other narrative genres to achieve economy. Other expressions of urgency reinforce these formulas and result in an almost dizzying narrative pace. The merchant must leave at daybreak *sanz plus targier* (28). His wife bids the clerc *Tot maintenant* (38) to be ready to slip into the house, and she wakes her husband with the words *Or sus!* (51), an exclamation repeated by the latter to his companion (93). The husband has slept *si longuement* (53) and *fait...trop grant demeure* (55) that he will scarcely arrive at the market on time. He dresses *Tost* (59) and leaves the house, for he has *grant besoig* (67) to set out. Once the couple comes together *Ne firent pas grant demorance Ne grant delai* (82-83) to undress. But all this haste is to no avail since the hour is far too early. Having retraced his steps the husband cries out in turn *Or sus! levez vos tost!* (119), and the startled clerc hides *Maintenant* (120) while the wife jumps back to bed with the merchant, also *Maintenant* (178). When morning comes the pace quickens again: the husband dresses *sanz plus de sejor* (192) and the clerc appears *isnelepas* (202.) Upon discovering the mistake the clerc *ne s'en fist pas proier...trop longuement* (231) to describe his breeches. Such expressions of urgency which punctuate the narrative are not significant when viewed in isolation, but the effect of their accumulation is striking. They function not only to impart a sense of narrative economy, but they move the action swiftly and impatiently with a feeling of vitality essential to the very nature of the fabliau. They bind together the various scenes in a surge toward the comic climax and thereafter diminish in number if not disappear altogether once the climax is reached.[20] Such artistic control, rather than being a sign of literary mediocrity as Bédier held (p. 347), is actually essential to the literary success of the work.[21]

---

[20] This same frenzied pace was noted by Thomas D. Cooke in another fabliau, "Formulaic Diction and the Artistry of *Le chevalier qui recovra l'amor de sa dame,*" *Romania* 94 (1973), 232-40. See also Cooke, p. 74, n. 9, for other examples of what the author calls "non-hesitation formulas" in the fabliaux.

[21] See Raymond Eichmann, "The Artistry of Economy in the Fabliaux," *Studies in Short Fiction* 17 (1980), 67-73.

5. *Language and Versification*

a. Table of Rhymes

The following table provides a convenient list of rhymes which forms the basis for the study of the author's language. They are grouped orthographically following the spelling of the tonic vowel or diphthong employed by the scribe. This procedure is not intended to yield the phonological state of the author's language; its aim is limited to grouping together the homophonous phonemes which the author paired in his couplets. Orthographic discrepancies are provided with cross-references when evidence clearly indicates a phoneme which is not reflected in the spelling (e. g. *eme* see *ame*), and justifications are found in the section on the author's language.

a	commanda: manda 38, veilla: esveilla 50, ia: oublia 122, apareilla: veilla 194, venra: tendra 250
aces	beçaces: places 354
ai	see *é*
aies	see *ees*
aige	saige: coraige 190
aille	see *eille*
ain	vilain: ain (HAMUM) 220
ainz	conpainz: sainz 94
aire	see *ere*
aise	mauvaise: desplaise 162, malaise: desplaise 300, baise: desplaise 342
ait	see *et*
ame	dame: ame 114, feme: dame 286

anbre	chanbre: remenbre 302
ance	contenance: demorance 82
anne	see *enne*
anz	quanz: marcheanz 268
art	part: Renart 238
as	pas: isnelepas 202
auce	chauce: hauce 306
az	laz: solaz 20
é	cité: verité 4, asené: amené 116, trouvé: prouvé 296, ferai: serai 346, volenté: plenté 350, afiné: finé 360
ee	enjornee: demoree 44, forsenee: escrīee 134, trouvee: provee 278, trouvee: blasmee 298
ees	braies: moies 218, enpruntees: boutees 252
eille	conseille: oraille 326
el	bordel: lordel 156
ele	apele: nouvele 112
eles	noveles: beles 316
embre	see *anbre*
eme	see *ame*
en	vos en: sen 160
endre	atendre: entendre 72

enne	penne: forsanne 276
ent	longuement: certainement 54, longuement: doucement 232, comment: seulement 248, argent: gent 272
er	apeler: aler 92, aler: celer 206, aler: parler 356
ere	faire: afaire 158, escritoire: ere 274
et	aguet: fait 10, vet: aguet 46, vait: fait 126, vait: plet 288, retret: tret 304
eu	see *ieu*
eure	demeure: eure 56, eure: secoure 102
ez	atornez: tornez 60, alez: acolez 74, levez: avez 90, forsenez: senez 100, tornez: alez 110, avez: savez 294
ié	marchié: descoschié 58, songié: gié 260, songié: congié 338
iees	bailliees: deliees 226
ief	chief: derechief 236
ien	rien: bien 234
ienz	laienz: caienz 318
ier	mengier: targier 28, despoillier: moillier 84, Richier: couchier 108, brisier: huschier 118, merveillier: veillier 188, braier: proier 230, mengier: païer 270, mostier: cordelier 314, cordelier: deslier 320
iers	volentiers: arriers 262

iez	esveilliez: apareilliez 40
ieu	geu: Dieu 216
i	esjoï: oï 36, midi: respondi 98, merci: ci 138, desmenti: menti 150, regehi: oï 244
ie	mie: endormie 30, aïe: malbaillie 136, amie: mie 146, oïe: esbahie 222, prie: die 228, esjoïe: die 264, hardie: esbahie 290, marie: Marie 344, jalousie: aisie 348, vie: chevie 358
ile	vile: Gile 152
in	matin: voisin 208
int	avint: revint 284
ir	garantir: mentir 14, tenir: venir 96
ire	matire: dire 6, sire: ire 52, 124, 180, 292, rire: tire 324
is	fis: esbahis 172, mespris: pris 200, avis: vis 212
ise	aprise: mise 18, mise: ocise 330
ises	prises: mises 334
ist	lit: delit 24, 140, dist: Jesucrist 64, 246, esbahist: dist 106, issist: dist 144, dit: aïst 204, 328
it	see *ist*
iz	avertiz: partiz 42
obe	robe: lobe 308

oi	moi: esmoi 142 (see also *ees* and *ere*)
oie	convoie: voie 62, veroie: estoie 164, joie: connoissoie 182, concevroie: avroie 256, oie: joie 336
oies	see *ees*
oig	besoig: loig 68
oigne	besoigne: aloigne 78
oir	concevoir: voir 254
oire	Loire: foire 34
oise	borjoise: cortoise 8, borgoise: poise 80
oit	savoit: avoit 26, amoit: covenoit 32
oiz	foiz: Croiz 170
ole	fole: parole 176
ome	prodome: some 48
on	maison: raison 210
onques	adonques: onques 76
ont	entrefont: sont 214
onte	honte: conte 16, 322
or	paor: freor 186, jor: sejor 192, seignor: desennor 196, hennor: menor 242, menor: signor 258
ors	amors: tors 12, cors: hors 66
ort	sort: hort 128, tort: aport 332

orz	torz: jorz 240
osche	see *ouche*
ost	tost: repost 120
ot	conplot: plot 88, sot: mot 132
ote	see *oute*
ouche	se couche: couche 86, cosche: farouche 130
oure	see *eure*
ous	espox: vos 148
oute	tote: boute 178
u	despendu: tendu 352
ue	desconvenue: avenue 198, vestue: issue 224
ues	pendues: rues 312
ueil	sueil: ueil 70
ui	connui: enui 174
uit	bruit: tuit 154, mïenuit: ennuit 166
uiz	enuiz: mïenuiz 104
un	geün: Meün 266
ure	cure: aventure 2, aventure: sainture 310
urent	reconurent: furent 280
us	plus: conclus 282

usse	conneüsse: fusse 184
ust	pleüst: geüst 22
uz	venuz: nuz 168, menuz: venuz 340

b. Versification

The verse form of *Les Braies au cordelier*, like the great majority of twelfth and thirteenth-century works in narrative verse, is that of the octosyllable with couplet rhyme. In conformity with the usage of the period the author broke the couplet freely (3, 5, 11, etc.) and frequently employed *enjambement* (27, 36, etc.); he had a real penchant for transitions between the two verses of a couplet (Rychner, I, 34). These techniques of octosyllabic verse composition, traced to the initiative of Chrétien de Troyes,[22] join with those features of composition and style noted above to produce a supple expression and lively movement of narrative events.

The author resorts to a minimum number of verse fillers (*chevilles*) and he never settles for assonance or imperfect rhyme (if we admit the emendation to *alez* in vs 110). He carefully avoids identical rhyme but does employ homonymic rhyme on two occasions: *se couche: couche* 86 and *marie: Marie* 344.[23] In the manner of Rutebeuf and Guillaume de Lorris he uses the "rime équivoque" *i a: oublia* 122,[24] and he consciously seeks rich and leonine rhyme which embrace more than one lexical item: *vos en: sen*

---

[22] Paul Meyer, "Le couplet de deux vers," *Romania* 23 (1894), 1-35: "Je me borne à dire que dans aucune des branches de *Renard*, dans aucun fabliau, dans aucun roman d'aventure du XIIIe siècle, le couplet n'est construit à la façon ancienne" (p. 25). Meyer points out further that in the thirteenth century the integrity of the couplet, in the old manner, is found especially in those passages where an author intended a tone of gravity or sententiousness (pp. 22-23), a situation unlikely to arise in a fabliau.

[23] A well-known figure of rhetoric termed *annominatio* (Faral, p. 93). On the distinction between "identical" and "homonymic" rhyme, see P. Rickard, "Semantic Implications of Old French Identical Rhyme," *Neuphilologisches Mitteilungen* 66 (1965), 355-401.

[24] The same rhyme is found five times in the second part of the *Roman de la Rose* (Langlois I, p. 174).

160, *de moi: esmoi* 142 (fall of *s* plus consonant). The author shows a fondness for rich and leonine rhyme, also a prescribed technique of the period,[25] although not perhaps to the degree that many poets of the mid-thirteenth century did. For the sake of convenience, I reduce Freymont's six categories to three:[26] sufficient (masculine and feminine, categories I and II), rich (III), and leonine (IV-VI). Of the 180 couplets which make up the *Braies*, 97 are sufficient, 38 rich, and 45 leonine, yielding percentages as follows: 53% sufficient, 21% rich, and 25% leonine. Although somewhat more conservative in exploiting these possibilities than either Guillaume de Lorris (38%, 23%, 39%) or Rutebeuf (38%, 12%, 50%), the author of the *Braies* does follow the ever-increasing tendency, towards the middle of the thirteenth century, to seek more than sufficient rhymes in verse composition.

c. Language of the Author

1. Nasal *e* and *a* are joined in rhyme: *chanbre: remenbre* 302, *feme: dame* 286, and if we admit leonine rhyme *garantir: mentir* 14. While *feme: dame* could rhyme in those texts where nasalized *e* and *a* are normally kept separate (Bastin, *Ysopets,* xxiii, and Buffum, *Violette,* p. xix),[27] this

---

[25] These rhymes were facilitated by such convenient techniques as pairing verbs of the same inflection (*concevroie: avroie* 256), morphological construction (*longuement: doucement* 232), or root (*desmenti: menti* 150).

[26] I follow here the procedure of E. Freymont, "Über den reichen Reim bei altfranzösischen Dichtern bis zum Anfang des XIV. Jahrh.," *Zeitschrift für romanische Philologie* 6 (1882), 1-36, 177-215, in not considering feminine rhyme as rich (which would yield percentages considerably higher). I term sufficient those rhymes involving homophony of the tonic vowel (or diphthong) and the following consonants, if any. Rich rhyme extends homophony to the pretonic consonant, leonine to the pretonic vowel and all following phonemes. In eight cases the author even manages *plus que léonine* rhyme (Freymont's category VI), but these are mostly of the type *afinè: finè* 360. The following pretonic vowels are considered to form leonine rhyme: *braier, proier* 230 on the basis of the rhyme *braies: moies* 218 (see below, p. 25); *garantir: mentir* 14 (see below); *paor: freor* 186; *avertiz: partiz* 42, cautiously assuming that *er* opened to *ar; aler: parler* 356, where assimilation of *r* to *l* is very probable as in part I of the *Roman de la Rose* (Langlois I, p. 268).

[27] Presumably owing to the denasalization of *feme>fame*.

feature of the author's language would in general exclude the Picard and Walloon regions (Gossen, *Grammaire*, § 15), and according to Langlois, I, p. 212, the mixture of such rhymes was even more widespread in the Orleanais than it is in Modern French.

2. The results of Latin long *o* and short *o* are joined in rhyme: *demeure: eure* 56,[28] *eure: secoure* 102. While Jean de Meung seems to make no distinction between close and open *o* (Langlois I, pp. 217-21), it is inadvisable to place too much importance on these rhymes owing to the frequent analogical fluctuations of the present stem of verbs of this class (one would expect *demore* or *demoure* and *secorre* or *secourre* at this date, but *demeure* and *querre* are attested, Bartsch, s.v. *secorre*). Even so, the sound issuing from Latin long and short *o* in the thirteenth century rhyme over a wide area of Northern France and are practically worthless for localizing a work.

3. The reduction of *-iee* (< palatal + -ATA) to *ie* (with stress on *i*) is frequently attested by the rhyme: *mie: endormie* 30, *aïe: malbaillie* 136, *oïe: esbahie* 222, *jalousie: aisie* 348. Usually traced to the North and East, this development is in fact attested over a wide area of the *Langue d'Oïl* where in the thirteenth century it was an accepted feature of the literary *koïnė* (Wacker, pp. 48-49). Gossen, § 8, notes that it was part of the vocalism of the South Eastern region, but Langlois I, pp. 235-36, rejects this development for the Orleanais. However, both parts of the *Roman de la Rose* contain such rhymes.

4. The result of Latin -ĔRIA is *-ire* in *dire: matire* 6, characteristic of Francien, Orleanais, Picard, and a part of Champagne but excluding Walloon, Northern Champenois, Burgundian, and the West (Gossen § 13). On the phonological development, see Fouché, *Phonétique*, II, 417-19. The same rhyme is found regularly in the *Roman de la Rose* (Langlois I, p. 156) and Rutebeuf (Bastin-Faral, I, 125).

5. Vowels in hiatus are retained: *marcheanz* 268, *meïsme* 284, *conceü* 337, *Meün* 33, etc., *paor* 185, *geün* 265 (note however that *Orliens* 3 is disyllabic). Part I of the *Roman de la Rose* shows no evidence of synaeresis, but in Jean de Meung contracted forms begin to appear (Langlois I, p. 279).

---

[28]The same rhyme is found in both parts of the *Roman de la Rose* (Langlois I, pp. 80, 149).

6. The diphthong *ië* is never reduced to *e*. Three rhymes in *er* of class Ia verbs are kept distinct from the nine in *ier* of class Ib. Langlois found no example of this reduction in part I of the *Roman de la Rose* and only a trace in Jean de Meung (Langlois I, p. 236).

7. On two occasions *oi* (whether from long *o* + yod or long *e* tonic free) rhymes with *e* (the result of the reduction of *ai* or the development of ERAT): *escritoire: ere* 274, *braies: moies* 218, and the leonine rhyme *braier: proier* 230.[29] The rhyme *moi: esmoi* 142 is in all probability not comparable since *esmoi* is a doublet of *esmai* and the word in Old French could rhyme with either *oi* or *ai* (*T.-L.*, III, 1105-06). It is possible that in *escritoire: ere* the rhyme is *e: we*, i.e., with the second element of the diphthong, and that long *o* + yod developed as it did in "standard" Old French (Langlois I, p. 194, n. 1 and Aurembou, p. 268). In the case of *braies: moies* the development *ai>e:e<ei<*long *e* tonic free is assured. In Jean de Meung this development is pervasive (Langlois I, pp. 198-99 and 211-12). Cf. *valeir: air, veire* (VERA): *necessaire, ameie: aie* (cited by Fouché, *Phonétique*, II, 271; cf. Pope, §1325, iv.).[30] Aurembou, p. 269, notes that in the Orleanais patois *we* (*<ei<*long *e*) alternates with *e* and that "D'une façon générale les plus jeunes emploient (we), les plus vieux (e)."

8. Fall of *s+t*: *dit: aïst* 204, 328 (but see n. 204), characteristic of both parts of the *Roman de la Rose* (Langlois I, pp. 247, 273-75).

9. *z* (< *ts*) > *s*: *amors: tors* 12, *fis* (FECI): *esbahis* 172, *enuiz: mïenuiz* 104. Although a development of Picard in the early period (Gossen, §40), the muting of the dental element of *z* became widespread in the thirteenth century (Wacker, p. 69). Both parts of the *Roman de la Rose* show the same development (Langlois I, p. 270).

---

[29]Langois I, p. 237, describes such pretonic (leonine) rhymes as follows: "Les rimes ne peuvent fournir de renseignements sur la voyelle de la pénultième syllabe que dans les terminaisons masculines, et uniquement si cette voyelle n'est séparée de la suivante par aucune consonne."

[30]And also in Guillaume de Lorris: *faire: voire* (Langlois I, p. 272).

10. *t* of past participles issuing from -ATUM is not attested: *songië: gië* 260.[31]

11. Survival of *h* in words of Germanic origin: *sa honte* 15, 241, *cele honte* 321.

12. Fall of *t* in the perfect 3 of weak verbs: *midi: respondi* 98.

13. The rhymes and meter reveal that the author adhered for the most part to the two-case system of Old French. Exceptions are *descoschië* 58 and *menuz* 339, both necessitated by the rhyme.

14. The reduced form *el* of the feminine pronoun is attested four times (14, 30, 127, 133), but there are nine occurrences of *ele*. This form, found widely in Old and Middle French texts (Nyrop, II, 401), is preferred by the authors of the *Roman de la Rose* (Langlois I, p. 291). Cf. Pope, §839.

15. Absence of analogical *e* in feminine adjectives of class II and adverbs: *grant* 55, 82, 197, etc., *tel* 345, *forment* 36.

16. Extension of analogical *s* in the nominative of *sires* 114, 142, 151, 158, but *sire* in rhyme with *ire* 51, 124, 179, 291. This double treatment of *sire* could be resolved by supposing the hiatus *sirë*, but it is much more probable that the author had both the older and newer forms at his disposal. In three of the four cases, *sire* functions as a vocative; *sires* is never so used.

17. The tonic form of the personal pronoun *gië* is attested in rhyme with *songië* 260.

18. There is no evidence of analogical *e* in the present indicative 1 of class I verbs: *aim* 171, *aport* 332. In the case of *conte* 16, it derives from a Latin proparoxyton (Fouché, *Verbe,* §87).

19. The present indicative 3 of *aler* is *vait / vet,* never *va* (in rhymes with *aguet* 46, *fait* 126, *plet* 288).

---

[31] This same rhyme is found in both parts of the *Roman de la Rose* (Langlois I, pp. 76, 141).

20. The forms *onques* 70, 171 and *encor* 104 are attested by the meter.

21. The subjunctive present 3 of *enoier* is *ennuit: mienuit* 166, a rhyme that Jean de Meung also employs (Langlois I, p. 333).

The language of the author as revealed by evidence of meter and rhyme shows few specific dialectal traits. The findings must remain all the more tenuous given the small number of couplets from which evidence of dialect is available. However, certain features of the author's language do seem to eliminate many regions of the *Langue d'Oïl*, while others point to the South Central dialect, that of Orleans: the rhyme of *an* and *en* (no. 1), the rhyme in the result of short and long *o* tonic free (no. 2), the reduction of *iee* to *ie* (no. 3), the rhyme *dire: matire* (no. 4), the retention of vowels in hiatus (no. 5), the absence of the reduction of *ie* to *e* (6), the loss of the dental element of *z* (no. 9), the prevalence of the reduced feminine pronoun *el* (no. 14), the absence of analogical *e* in the feminine adjectives of the *grant* type (no. 15), and the absence of analogical forms of class I verbs (no. 18), all are found in the Orleanais of the thirteenth century. But most important, the reduction of *ei* (< long *e* tonic free) to *e* (no. 7) indicates specifically the South Central region.

There is then evidence to suggest that the author of *Les Braies au cordelier* may well have originated, like the authors of the *Roman de la Rose*, from the area of Orleans and that his language discloses certain features of that dialect. But it is evident too that he possessed considerable literary skill, and he drew presumably on usages prevalent over a much wider area of thirteenth-century France: he exploited features of a composite literary language sanctioned by writers of his time from many regions.

d. Language of the Scribe

The scribal characteristics of the base manuscript have been described many times in connection with the numerous works preserved in it. T.B.W. Reid, *Twelve Fabliaux from MS F. Fr. 19152 of the Bibliothèque Nationale* (Manchester, 1958), pp. xvi-xxi, has given a detailed description of the scribe's language. Reid rejects previously held opinions that the scribe exhibits a marked Picard tendency in the form of words except in those texts of Northern provenance, and he concludes that the orthographic features point toward the South-Central or South-Eastern regions and that most are attested for the *Roman de la Rose* (p. xviii). To facilitate the reading of the text I present here those peculiarities of the language of MS D which are either slightly unusual or which depart from "standard" Old French usage.

ai for *a* before *-ge* and *-che*: *saige* 8, 189, *coraige* 26, 190, *saiche* 14.

o more often than *eu* < close *o* tonic free: *menor* 257, etc.; but *eure* (HORA) 101, etc.

i once for *ei* + palatal *n*: *signor* 258.

ai once for *ei*+ palatal *l*: *oraille* 326.

a for *ai* in *sa* (SAPIO) 54 (see note).

Pretonic *o* weakened to *e*: *hennor* 241, *desennor* 196.

an for *en*: *forsanne* 276 (but *forsenee* 133), *an* (INDE) 152, *pranre* 271.

ei for *ai* + nasal: *seinte* 170.

ie for *iee* (< palatal + -ATA): *endormie* 30, etc. This form is found consistently in rhyme, but within a verse the Francien *-iee* is more prevalent: *enlaciee* 19, *liee* 81, etc.

g for *ch*: *guenges* 12.

Absence of glide consonants in secondary groups: *venrroiz* 56, *venront* 154, *venra* 249, and inversely *pranre* 271.

Fall of *s* + consonant: *beau sire* 51, 179, *soupeçon* 347, *un clers* 7, *Lor vient* 111. The muting of *s* is further attested by its adventitious appearance in such words as *Mestre* 1, *descoschië* 58, *cosche* 129, *huschier* 118.

Occasional doubling of intervocalic consonant: *forsanne* 276, *penne* 275, *venrroiz* 56.

Loss of the dental in *z* (<*ts*): *tors* 12 (but *torz* 239, *jorz* 240, *toz* 94, etc.).

n often for *m* + labial: *conplot* 87, *chanbre* 301, *conpainz* 93, *remenbre 302*.

g for *ng* representing palatal *n* (see n. 67): *besoig* 67, *loig* 68, *tieg* 175, but when intervocalic *gne: besoigne: aloigne* 78.

s for *ss: ausi* 133.

Fall of *l* + consonant: *ce* = *cel* 17.

Retention of etymological future 5 endings: *venrroiz* 56, *feroiz* 189.

Analogical *s* in class II nouns: *li autres 98*.

Possessive pronoun of the Norman type: *mis* 151, 158.

Metathesis of the future stem: *couverra* 234.

poi (PAUCUM) always for *pou*, 276, 330, 343.

The oblique plural once for the nominative: *voisins* 154.

Absence of analogical *e* in class II feminine adjectives: *tel* 15, *grant* 55, 82, 197.

Feminine tonic pronoun *lui* for *li* 213.

Absence of analogical *e* in present 1 of class I verbs: *commant* 64, *aim* 171, *aport* 332.

Absence of analogical *s* in present 1 of verbs: *di* 79, 107, *sui* 136, etc., *sai* 267, *tieg* 175.

Omission of *e* of feminine past participles: *pris'* 220, *mal'* 309.

Scribe always writes *riens* (except in rhyme with *bien* 233) whether nominative 25 or oblique 31, 298, 299. See n. 25.

C'EST LI ROMANZ DES BRAIES

120*f*
   Mestre vueil m'entente et ma cure
   A raconter une aventure
   Qu'avint a Orliens la cité;
   Ce testmoigne par verité   4
   Cil qui m'en dona la matire.
   Il avint si con j'oï dire
   C'un[s] clers amoit une borjoise
   Qui molt estoit saige et cortoise;   8
   Molt savoit d'enging et d'aguet.
   A feme qui tel mestier fait
   Et qui velt amer par amors
   Couvient savoir guenges et tors   12
   Et enging por soi garantir:
   Bien covient qu'el saiche mentir
   Tel ore por covrir sa honte.
   La borjoise dont ge vos conte   16
   Fu bien de ce mestier aprise.
   Comme cele qu'Amors ot mise
   Et bien enlaciee en ses laz
   Molt ama du clerc le solaz.   20
   Molt vosist et molt li pleüst
   Qu'antre ses braz toz nuz geüst,
   Et ele o lui en un beau lit
   Por avoir du clerc le delit.   24
   Li sires qui riens ne savoit
   Quel coraige sa feme avoit
   Li dist un soir aprés mengier
   Qu'au point du jor, sanz plus targier,   28
   L'esveillast, ne l'obliast mie,
   Et qu'el ne fust trop endormie

Rejected Readings of D: 23 cele se jut en—un jor a.

—*A Variants*: 2 a fere .i. dit dune a.—5 il avint si con joi dire—6 si c. je truis en la matire—14 c. que s.—15 o. est p.—17 de cel m.—20 M. amast dun c.—21 v. bien et li p.—27 a dit au s.—28 s. atargier—29 L'e. quel nel lessast m.

>
> S'ele de riens son preu amoit.
> Au jor lever le covenoit
> Por aler a Meün sor Loire
> Ou il avoit marchié et foire.
> La borgoise molt s'esjoï
> Forment quant la parole oï
> Que ses sires li commanda.
> Tot maintenant au clerc manda
> Qu'il fust la nuit bien esveilliez
> [Et qu'il fust bien apareilliez]
> D'entrer come bien avertiz
> Laienz quant en sera partiz
> Li sires devant l'enjornee.
> Que vos feroie demoree?
> Mais li borgois couchier se vet,
> Et la dame fu en aguet
> Et en grant porpens du prodome
> D'esveillier au premerain some.
> Il dormi et ele veilla;
> Et quant li sires s'esveilla,
> Ele li dit: "Or sus! beau sire,
> Certes, molt ai au cuer grant ire
> Que nos avons si longuement
> Dormi. Ge sa certainement
> Que fait avez trop grant demeure;
> A peine venrroiz mais a eure
> Hui mais a Meün au marchié."
> Lors s'est li borjois descoschié,
> Tost fu vestuz et atornez,
> De son ostel s'en est tornez;
> Et la borgoise le convoie
> Sanz plus jusqu'a l'uis de la voie.
> A l'issir de laienz li dist:

121*a*

32
36
40
44
48
52
56
60

42 q. il s.—43 desires d.—46 mais la

---

34 m. ou f.—35 b. sen e.—43 lajornee—45 que li b. c. sen v.—46 en bon point—49 et cele v.—51 dist—55 Q. t. a. f. g.—58 li preudom d.—59 si sest v.

32   Les Braies au cordelier

          "Ge vos commant a Jesucrist   64
          Qui soit garde de vostre cors."
             Atant li borgois s'en ist hors
          Qui avoit d'errer grant besoig.
          Lors ne fu pas d'ilueques loig   68
          Quant li clers a passé le sueil
          Qui onques n'ot dormi de l'ueil
          De tote la nuit por atendre,
          Si comme vos poez entendre.   72
          Quant li sires s'en fu alez,
          Lors fu li clers plus acolez
          Et quatre tanz baisiez adonques
          Que li borgois n'ot esté onques   76
          Qui or s'en vait en sa besoigne.
          Que vos feroie plus d'aloigne?
121b   Mais ge vos di que la borgoise
          Et li clers a qui point n'en poise   80
          Firent molt liee contenance;
          Ne firent pas grant demorance
          Ne grant delai au despoillier.
          Li clers toz nuz o la moillier   84
          Au borgois, qui s'en vait, se couche,
          Braz a braz jurent en la couche.
          La borgoise ama le conplot,
          Si fist du clerc ce que li plot.   88
             Et li borgois qui fu levez
          Trop tost, si comme oï avez,
          Ala un preudom' apeler
          Qui devoit ovuec lui aler,   92
          Et li dist: "Or sus! beax conpainz,
          Tant avons dormi, par toz Sainz,
          Que por fox nos poons tenir;
          Ainz qu'a Meün puission venir   96

66 se mist h.—73 que li s. s'en fust a.—90 si t. c. (-1)
----
66 li preudom sen i. fors—67 quar d'e. a. g.—68 il ne—73 li preudom s'en—
78 f. longue a.—80 a cui p.—83 g. dolor au—85 s'en va se—86 j. sus la—88
du c. si f. ce q. lui p.—91 A. son voisin a.

Sera il bien pres de midi."
Et li autres li respondi:
"Conpainz, estes vos forsenez?
Vos n'estes mie bien senez 100
Qui volez errer a tel eure.
Beax conpainz, se Diex me secoure
Et gart mon cors de toz enuiz,
Il n'est pas encor mïenuiz." 104
—Conpainz, fait cil qui s'esbahist,
Dites vos voir?" Et cil li dist:
"Ge vos di voir, par saint Richier!"
—Ge me vois donc, fait il, couchier." 108
Atant s'en est d'iluec tornez,
A son ostel s'en est alez;
Lor[s] vient a l'uis et si apele.
Diex! con ci a male nouvele! 112
"Beax douz amis, ce dit la dame,
Mes sires est a l'uis, par m'ame;
Nos somes molt mal asené!
Deables le ront amené 116
Qui li puissent le col brisier!"
Et cil ne fine de huschier
Et dist: "Or sus! levez vos tost!"
Maintenant li clers se repost 120
Et prist quanque du sien i a
Fors ses braies qu'il oublia

121*c* Dont tuit troi orent puis grant ire.
Tant apela a l'uis li sire 124
Qu'entrez i est, couchier se vait,
Et la dame l'endormi fait.
Cil l'apela, el fist le sort

---

110 o. est repairiez—119 l. luis t.—123 ires—124 sires—125 tantost .i. poi c.

---

102 B. amis se D. me sequere—103 Et il me g. de—108 je men v.—111 dont fiert a.—112 a pesme n.—113 a. ca d.—115 malement s. a.—116 maufe lont si tost ramene—124 l'u. ses s.—127 l'a. bien f.

Con cele qui molt sot de hort. 128
Li borgois delez li se cosche,
Et cele qui fist le farouche
Por tenir le vilain por sot
Sailli du lit sanz dire mot 132
Ausi con s'el fust forsenee;
A haute voiz s'est escrïee:
"Sainte Marie, aïe! aïe!
Ge sui trahie et malbaillie 136
Se vos n'avez de moi merci."
Et puis a dit: "Qui est ce ci
Qui s'est couchiez dedenz mon lit?
Ja nus hom soulaz ne delit 140
Fors mon seignor n'avra de moi."
Lors fu li sires en esmoi
Que sa feme du sens n'issist;
Au plus soef qu'il pot li dist: 144
"Bele tres douce chiere amie,
Por Dieu ne vos marisiez mie;
Ge sui vostre loiax espox
Qui couchiez m'estoie lez vos." 148
Et ele l'en a desmenti.
"Vos avez, fait ele, menti:
Mis sires est hors de la vile;
Alez vos an ou, par saint Gile, 152
Ge crïerai ja a tel bruit
Que noz voisin i venront tuit.
Il n'a mie caienz bordel."
Molt fist bien le putain lordel 156
La dame qui bien le sot faire.
"Mis sires est en son afaire,
Fait el, alez, ralez vos en!
Molt estes fox et hors du sen 160

---

154 voisins—159 el a luiz r.

———

128 icel q.—130 q. molt fu fa.—131 v. a s.—133 c. se fust f.—136 or s. je morte et—138 qui est ce couchiez delez mi—139 Q. est entrez d.—142 en esfroi—147 leal—148 Q. m'e. c. l.—151 e. fors de—158 e. a son a.—160 vos e.

Qui m[e] cuidiez faire mauvaise."
—Dame, fait il, ne vos desplaise,
Preude feme estes et veroie;
Certes, trop tost levez estoie: 164
Il n'est pas plus de mïenuit.
Si vos pri que ne vos ennui
121d Se ge sui arrieres venuz;
Delez vos me couchai toz nuz 168
Con cil qui l'ai fet mainte foiz.
Si m'aïst Diex et seinte Croiz,
Mielz vos aim c'onques mais ne fis."
—Sire, fait ele, or m'esbahis 172
De ce qu' ançois ne vos connui.
Ge vos en ai fait grant enui;
Ge m'en tieg ore molt por fole.
Or vos connois a la parole; 176
Certes, ge m'en esbahis tote."
Maintenant delez lui se boute,
Si l'acole, puis dit: "Beau sire,
Por Dieu, pardonez moi vostre ire, 180
Que ja, se de vos aie joie,
Que ge pas ne vos connoissoie.
Sachiez, se ge vos conneüsse,
Ja du lit issue ne fusse. 184
Mais j'avoie d'autre paor;
Se g'[en] estoie en grant freor,
Ne vos en devez merveillier.
Mestier n'avez de plus veillier; 188
Dormez, vos si feroiz que saige."
Et cil qui en ot grant coraige
Si dormi jusqu'au point du jor.
 Au matin sanz plus de sejor 192
Se vesti et apareilla,
Et la borgoise qui veilla
Commanda a Dieu son seignor.

---

195 commande a (-1).
___
166 p. quil ne—175 et si m'en t. or m.—179 l'a. et li dist B.—181 se je de v. joieuse soie—183 et S. se v.—184 l. levee ne—186 si en es.—188 n'a. M. de—190 ot bon co.—191 dormi jusques au.

Mais ne set pas la desennor 196
Ne la tres grant descouvenue
Que li est cel jor avenue,
Quar li sires a si mespris
Que les braies au clerc a pris; 200
N'il meïsme ne le set pas.
Et li clers vint isnelepas
A la dame, si li a dit:
"Bele amie, se Diex m'aïst, 204
Orendroit m'en covient aler.
Qui aime il doit s'amor celer;
Por ce m'en vueil aler matin
Que ne me voient li voisin 208
Hors issir de vostre maison."
—Beax amis, vos dites raison,

121*e*   Dist la dame, ce m'est avis."
La bouche li baise et le vis, 212
Et il a li, puis s'entrefont
Le gieu por quoi assemblé sont.
Et quant il orent fait lor geu,
Si s'entrecommandent a Dieu. 216
Lors prist li clers les autres braies,
Puis dit: "Ce ne sont pas les moies,
Ainz sont les braies au vilain."
Bien est la dame pris' a l'ain! 220
  Quant el a la parole oïe,
Molt malement fu esbahie.
Sa robe a en son dos vestue,
Puis s'en est de son lit issue. 224
Au clerc a tex braies bailliees
Qui sont bones et deliees;
Par amors li commande et prie
Que toz les garnemanz li die 228

213 a lui p.
―――――
198 que c. j. li e. a.—199 que ses s. a—209 i. fors de—220 B. fu la—222 M. fu dolente et e.—225 c. autres br. baillies—226 Q. furent blanches et delies—227 P. amor li requiert et p.—228 t. ses g.

         Qui pendoient a son braier.
         Et il ne s'en fist pas proier,
         Ce m'est avis, trop longuement,
         Ainz li a dit molt doucement.   232
         Lors dist qu'ele n'en doute rien;
         Ele se couverra molt bien,
         Bien en savra venir a chief.
         Lors s'entrebaisent derechief;   236
         Atant li clers d'iluec s'en part.
         La dame sot molt de Renart,
         Engigneuse fu de toz torz.
         Quant [il] fu grant eure et grant jorz,   240
         Por changier sa honte a hennor
         S'en vint a un frere menor,
         Si li dist et li regehi
         Tot ce que vos avez oï   244
         Et li prie por Jhesucrist
         Qu'il li aïst, et il li dist:
         "Dame, por Dieu, et ge comment?"
         —Dites, fait ele, seulement   248
         A mon seignor, quant il venra,
         Qui por mauvese me tendra,
         Que vos braies ai enpruntees
         Et desoz ma coite boutees   252
         Por filz ou fille concevoir,
         Quar j'avoie songié por voir
121f   Que ge cele nuit concevroie
         Enfant, quant en mon lit avroie   256
         Les braies d'u[n] frere menor.
         Sire, fait el, a mon signor
         Dites que j'ai ainsi songié."
         —Dame, fait il, si ferai gié   260

239 toz jorz—260 il molt volentiers
———
230 Et cil nen f. mie dangier—234 quele sen chevira m.—240 Q. il fu g. e. de j.—241 P. chacier sa—247 Da. dist il et—251 b. en ai portees —252 coute—255 Q. ce. n. conceveroie—256 .i. E. quen m.—260 sachiez bien que si f.

De molt bon gre et volentiers."
Atant s'en vet la dame arriers
Qui de ce fu molt esjoïe.
    Or est raison que ge vos die   264
Du borgois qui fu a geün
Venuz au marchié de Meün,
Et autres o lui ne sai quanz.
Li borgois comme marcheanz   268
Ala o les autres mengier;
Quant vint a son escot païer,
Si cuida pranre son argent,
Si con tesmoignent mainte gent,   272
[Si] a trové une escritoire
Ou li quanivez au clerc ere
Et son parchemin et sa penne.
Par poi li borgois ne forsanne   276
Quant il sa borse n'a trouvee.
Lors apele putain provee
Sa feme; ce me reconnurent
Aucun qui en la place furent.   280
Que vos diroie de ce plus?
Molt fu esbahiz et conclus
De ce que li quas li avint.
Cel jor meïsme s'en revint   284
A son ostel; quant vit sa feme,
Lors li a dit: "Par mon chief, dame!
Or sai ge bien comment il vait;
Enpirié avez vostre plet."   288
Et la dame qui fu hardie
Et qui ne fu pas esbahie
Li dist hardiement: "Beax sire,
N'aiez en vostre cuer tel ire;   292

---

273 trove a u. (-1)—285 A sont o.

---

262 va—265 q. toz fu g.—266 v. cu m.—267 Et dautres o l.—270 Q. ce v. a lescot p.—277 il na sa b. t.—278 L. lapele p.—279 *om*—280 *om*—282 confus—283 ce quilueques li—284 celui j. m. s'en vint—286 dites moi fet il bone da.—287 vous savez b.—290 qui ne fu p. trop e.—292 c. grant i.

	Ge sai molt bien que vos avez,	
	La verité pas ne savez	
	De ce que vos avez trouvé.	
	Bien vos sera por voir prouvé	296
	Que de chose qu'aiez trouvee	
	Ne doi estre de riens blasmee.	
122*a*	Ne soiez de riens en malaise,	
	Mais venez, et ne vos desplaise,	300
	Ovueques moi dedanz ma chanbre."	
	Et il i vait et li remenbre	
	Tot ce que ge vos ai retret.	
	Et cil les braies au clerc tret	304
	D'entor lui et les soes chauce.	
	Maintenant la dame li hauce	
	Et lieve les pans de la robe;	
	Comme cele qui bien le lobe	308
	Et set assez mal' aventure	
	Li a mises a la sainture	
	Les braies au clerc et pendues,	
	Porter li fist aval les rues	312
	Jusqu' atant qu'il vint au mostier,	
	La ou erent li cordelier.	
	Par tans orra autres noveles	
	Que ne li seront pas molt beles.	316
	Tantost con il entra laienz,	
	Si dist: "A il nul[ui] caienz	
	Qui m'ensaignast tel cordelier?"	
	Et cil qui devoit deslïer	320
	La borgoise de cele honte,	
	Dont vos avez oï le conte,	
	S'est levez et commance a rire.	
	Tantost a une part le tire,	324

304 cl. let—305 de son dos les s. si c.—318 Cil li d.

---

299 *om*—300 *om*—301 or venez o m. en ma—307 de sa r.—312 quil porta a meun vestues—313 portez les sire au cordelier—314 tout maintenant sanz delaier—315 *om*—316 *om*—317 si tost comme il—324 maintenant dune p.

Trestot ce li dist et conseille
Tot coiement dedenz l'oraille
Que la borjoise li a dit.
"Sire, fait cil, se Diex m'aïst, 328
Grant joie m'avez el cuer mise;
Par poi que n'ai ma feme ocise
Par mon pechié et a grant tort.
Sire, voz braies vos aport: 332
Vez les ci." Et il les a prises,
En une aumoire les a mises,
Puis li dist, que li borjois l'oie,
Que Diex li doint avoir a joie 336
Conceü ce qu'el a songié.
"Amen!" fist cil. Lors prist congié
Li borgois au frere menuz,
A son ostel s'en est venuz; 340
Lors acole sa feme et baise,
Puis dist: "Dame, ne vos desplaise
S'un poi vos ai faite marie;
Foi que ge doi sainte Marie 344
Tel amende vos en ferai
Que ja mais de vos ne serai
En soupeçon de jalousie."
   Or est la dame bien aisie 348
De faire au clerc sa volenté,
Que por s'amor a grant plenté
Ot mis du sien et despendu.
Bien a la borgoise tendu 352
Au borgois le sac as beçaces.
En toz leus et en totes places
Porra mais venir et aler,
Que ja n'en osera parler 356

---

326 trestot belement en l'o.—335 P. le d.

---

328 f. il se—333 Et cil les—335 P. a dit q.—336 Q. il li—338 prent—339 menu—340 o. en est venu—342 dame dist il ne—343 se je v.—348 e. bien la d. aaisie—350 qui por—352 b. rendu—356 n'en estovra p.

Li cox ja mais jor de sa vie.
Bien s'est la borgoise chevie,
Molt a bien son plait afiné.
Atant ai mon flabel finé. 360

Explicit

---

359 qui bien et bel s. p. define—360 A. m. fablel ici fine—explicit des braies au cordelier (*in a later hand*)

NOTES

3. *Qu'avint*: it is impossible to know whether this is a contraction of *qui* or whether it is a contraction of *que* with nominative function (see Ménard, § 64, 1 and Tobler, *Mélanges*, p. 156, n. 1). It is also possible that, before an impersonal verb, the construction should be considered *que il avint* with *il* not expressed which entails the normal contraction of *que* (see the remarks of Roach, *Continuations*, I, n. 1231). Cf. . .*noveles Que ne li seront pas molt beles* (316) where *Que* functions as a subject relative pronoun. See now the important discussion of *que* as subject pronoun in Harris, pp. 206-07.

7. *c'un*: in view of *clers, un* is not an oblique with nominative function, but an example of the fall of *s* + consonant.

11. *amors*, with *s* in the oblique singular, illustrates Frappier's "règle de l's." The frequency of this form is shown to increase steadily from the twelfth through the first half of the thirteenth century, culminating in the first part of the *Roman de la Rose* where it is found with absolute consistency (p. 452). It first appeared in the literature of *fin' amors*, and it quickly came to designate the specific love of courtly refinement which emerged from the romance and lyric. What is of interest here, of course, is the discrepant tone it establishes between a technical term of refined sensibility and the context depicted here. Although its occurrence in the fabliaux is common (Nykrog, p. 74), Frappier neglected *par amors* in the non-courtly literature of the period.

12. *savoir guenges et tors*, a common expression "to know twists and turns," whence "to know tricks and guiles." Cf.: *Tant me faites e tourz e ganches* (*Rose*, 8859) and *Ja set molt de tors et de gances* (*Perceval*, 5348). See *T.-L.*, IV, 727-28, which records this passage from the *Braies*.

15. *Tel ore*, "many a time, time after time" (*T.-L.*, X, 160).

17. *ce* = *cel*, with *l* deleted + consonant.

22. The subject of *geüst* is the clerk: "That he might lie naked...". On the well-known usage of *tot* employed adverbially but which continues to

inflect, see Ménard, § 32, 2.

25. The scribe writes regularly *riens* in the oblique singular in conformity with Old French usage (cf. vss 31, 298, 299), although the only form certain for the author is *rien* (233). Various explanations have been advanced to explain this *s*, the most probable being the fact that the nominal function of *rien* is difficult to distinguish from its adverbial one, accounting for the spread of *s* as an adverb marker even to those cases where *riens* is clearly a direct object. See the discussion by Brian Woledge, "La flors et la flor: La déclinaison des féminins chez Chrétien de Troyes," in *Marche Romane: Mélanges. . .Wathelet-Willem* (Liège, 1978), pp. 717-40, esp. 725-29.

26. *Quel coraige sa feme avoit,* "what was on his wife's mind." *Coraige* is well attested with the meaning of "disposition of mind or intention."

31. *S'ele. . .son preu amoit,* "If she knew what was good for her."

32. Although occasionally in Old French *couvenir* governs the dative, it is most common as here for it to take a direct object pronoun (cf. Tobler, *Mélanges,* pp. 113, 272).

41. *come bien avertiz,* an elliptical construction for *come [cil qui fu] bien avertiz,* "as one who has been well forewarned."

44. Such devices of narrative abridgement are formulaic clichés widespread in medieval narrative. On this *brevitas* topos as advocated by classical and medieval rhetorical theory, see Curtius, pp. 487-94.

45. *Mais* provides no more than a weak transition following the narrator's intervention and is therefore not adversative (Antoine, p. 1123: "on trouverait des textes où *mais* n'est presque plus qu'une pure transition."). Foulet, *Roland,* p. 419, glosses *mais,* which provides a transition to laisse 33 of the *Roland,* as "or," and Bédier, *Chanson de Roland, Commentaire,* p. 210, understands it as "et voici que," either of which would be appropriate here.

47. I have found no other example in Old French of the noun object of a dependent infinitive introduced by *de*. One would expect either *estre en porpens d'esveillier le prodome* or *estre en porpens du prodome esveillier.* Tobler, *Mélanges,* pp. 6-24, does treat at length the

problem of the logical subject of verbs introduced by *de* (i.e., the type *Mout est grans cose de prodomme*), and Gamillscheg, *Syntax*, p.268, gives examples of the Modern French *être de son devoir de faire*, but neither seems applicable here. It is possible that this is a variant of the well-attested construction where an infinitive, separated from the preposition which governs it, is introduced by *a* (i.e., *De son corps a ochirre fu chascuns desirans*; see Nyrop, V, 80, Livingston, p. 68, and the numerous examples in *T.-L.*, I, 23). But it seems more probable that this is a conflation of two constructions, *estre en porpens du prodome* and *estre en porpens d'esveillier*, which entailed a redundant *de*.

54. While some editors consider the reduction of *ai* to *a* in the first person a scribal lapse and correct it accordingly (e.g., *Respit*, p. cxxxix, Roach, *Continuations*, III, Pt. 1, 6161, etc., Reid, p. 3, vs 32 [a text edited from ms *D*], *Narcisse*, 860), others consider it an acceptable dialectal form and allow it to stand (e.g., *Tristan*, I, 337, 31, *Moniage*, 5750, *Lancelot do Lac*, II, 49). See the references in *Bliocadran*, n. 115, Pope, p. 488, vii, and Nyrop, II, 166. While most deal with the future 1 of verbs, the situation is analogous in the present and perfect endings. Fouché, *Verbe*, § 74, explains the development as the result of the absorption of the yod by the palatal in inversion, *sai ge* > *sa ge*, while Gossen, *Grammaire*, § 6, attributes it to the Picard dialect where there was a strong accent on the *a* of descending diphthongs.

67. Despite the forms *besoig: loig*, the diphthong is presumed to be nasalized. According to Ruelle, *Besant*, n. 3523, a correction to *besoi[n]g* is not advisable: "L'étude du phénomène et surtout de sa répartition n'est pas facilitée par les 'corrections' apportées par les éditeurs à la graphie *-oig-*."

81. *Faire liee contenance* is clearly synonymous with *faire chiere liee* 'to put on a happy face, to appear joyful;' cf. the example in *T.-L.*, II, 761, where both are joined in the same verse. Despite the failure of Godefroy or the *T.-L.* to record *contenance* with the meaning 'face,' and Jean Renson, *Les dénominations du visage en français*, II, p. 427, who concludes that ". . .le sens de 'visage'. . .peut paraître douteux," it is preferable to attribute this meaning to it here (rather than 'expression' or 'demeanor') as did Foulet, *Roland*, p. 358, in the much-discussed occurrence of the word in vs 830 of the *Roland* (see

the detailed note in *Chanson de Roland*, Brault, II, n. to vs 830). Diekmann, p. 4, merely repeats for *contenance* in the *Braies* the gloss of the *FEW*, II, 1106: "manière de se conduire, de se tenir vis-à-vis de qn." On the entire question see now Glyn Burgess, "Old French *contenance* and *contenant*" in Raymond J. Cormier, *Voices of Conscience* (Philadelphia, 1977), pp. 21-41.

82. *Ne firent...despoillier*, 'It didn't take them very long to strip,' with the infinitive employed substantively.

86. *couche*, "terme plus général que *lit* et qui implique souvent qqch. de temporaire ou d'imprévu" (Foulet, *Glossaire*, p. 52). But here it is obviously the conjugal bed in question and the author does not seem to make a distinction between *lit* (23 *et passim*) and *couche*.

87. Godefroy, II, 209, lists only two examples of *conplot*, but only this passage from the *Braies* with the meaning "lutte amoureuse" (wrongly attributed to *Des Tresces*), whence this single example in the *T.-L.*, II, 633, "Liebeskampf."

95. The pronoun *nos* is the object of *tenir*, not the subject of *poons*: "we can consider ourselves mad."

110. The correction is necessitated by the faulty rhyme.

115. The *T.-L.*, I, 579, gives only this example of *malement asené* from *A* (and none of *male asené*) and glosses it "übel bestellt", "to be in a bad way, fix." It is possible that *mal* should be considered a bound prefix (cf. *malbaillie* 136), though the *T.-L.* does not list it as a separate lexical item.

116. The omission of the definite article before *deables*, singular and plural, was common in Old French: cf. *Et quant deiables les i avoient menez* (*Joseph d'Arimathie*, 5-6; see also *Violette*, n. 5298). Although a correction to *deable* would make it consistent with the regular masculine paradigm, as a collective noun it is often found with or without *s* marker in the nominative plural, and hence it was allowed to stand; cf. *tuit deiables sont choses esperitex* (*Lancelot do Lac*, 22.30); see the discussion by Wolfgang, *Bliocadran*, n. 758.

124. It is curious that the husband first knocked at the door (presumably to give the clerc time to depart) then simply walked into the house (125). Le Grand d'Aussy (Appendix 5) perceived the difficulty and so invented a character, the servant, to open the door.

125. *Tantost* is an obvious example of the scribe's weakness for copying from previous lines (see vss 46 and 326). The correction was deemed all the more necessary since *Tant* would normally call for the correlative *que*.

126. Constructions like *faire l'endormi, faire le sort* (127), *faire le farouche* (130), and *faire le putain lordel* (156) are curious in that the attribute, with nominal function, often remains uninflected in Old French regardless of the subject. Tobler, *Mélanges*, p. 217, suggested the following explanation: "en désignant le rôle qu'on dit être joué par une personne, on n'a eu, à l'origine, nul égard au genre de cette personne" (see also the remark of Henry, *Cleomadès*, n. 7068). When however the attribute is clearly adjectival, the normal agreement ensues: cf. *estre endormie* (30) and *se faire mauvaise* (161).

131. As Nykrog observed (p. 127), *vilain* describes not only a social reality, but it often had a moral connotation. There is no doubt that the husband belongs to the class of tradesmen and possesses a house in Orleans. The two references to him as *vilain* (also 219), the first by the author and the second by the clerk, serve only to express contempt for him.

144. *Au plus soef qu'il pot*, 'In the softest (voice) possible.' On this expression, see Tobler, *Mélanges*, pp. 222-23.

152. Oaths on the saints commonly added a popular tone to the dialogue and, more often than not, were chosen for the necessity of the rhyme or as a verse filler. There is a possibility however that the choice was made with some care either to add local color (cf. *seinte Croiz* 170) or to serve as an allusion, sometimes humorous, to the narrative situation, its "thematic significance" in the words of Robert J. Blanch, "The Game of Invoking Saints in *Sir Gawain and the Green Knight,*" *American Benedictine Review* 31 (1980), 237. The reference to Saint Giles is perhaps a case in point: in addition to his connection with commercial activity (Blanch, p. 253), Giles was patron saint of lepers and thus he became, by the analogy of sin and disease, the

patron of lechers (leprosy was widely thought to increase sexual activity). An attribute of the saint was the herb fennel, long believed to be both an aphrodisiac and a cure for sterility in women (F. G. Holweck, *A Biographical Dictionary of the Saints* [London, 1924], p. 22). If the name of Giles were associated with lechery on the one hand and barrenness on the other, the invocation would be particularly apposite. See Ann S. Haskell, *Essays on Chaucer's Saints* (The Hague-Paris, 1976), pp. 26-31.

154. *voisins* is a scribal inadvertence; cf. the correct nominative plural in vs 208.

156. The comparatively rare adjective *lordel* (diminutive of *lort* < LURIDUM) is one of only two examples recorded by the *T.-L.*, V, 658, glossed "einfältig" (see also the *FEW*, V, 466a, "niais"). Of the two examples listed by Godefroy, V, 40, the second also qualifies *putain: Bien meschiez le putain lordel*, but the reference to B. N. *fr.* 837, f. 82r° is erroneous since the verse does not occur there, nor in the entire text of the *Lai d'Aristote* (folios 80v°—83 r°) in 837. This suggests that it is a garbled version of the verse from the *Braies* in ms *A*.

161. Although *Quim* is an acceptable contraction, I have emended it in order to restore the octosyllable.

164. It is tempting to emend to *levez [m]'estoie* to replace a passive construction with a pronominal one. There is however no support in *A* for such an emendation. On this use of the passive for the pronominal, see Sneyders de Vogel, § 167, where the passive, and precisely the verb *lever*, reflects directly the Latin *levatus sum* 'je me suis levé' (p. 10). See the detailed study of the development *levez est* > *levez s'est* in Anna Granville Hatcher, *Reflexive Verbs: Latin, Old French, Modern French* (Baltimore, 1942), pp. 133-38, and *Besant*, n. 2528.

170. The cathedral of the ancient see of Orleans was dedicated to Sainte-Croix. The construction of the Gothic edifice was completed by 1288 (and destroyed by the Huguenots in 1562). Contemporary then with the *Braies*, it is quite possible that this oath referred, not specifically to the Holy Cross, but to the new cathedral in Orleans currently under construction.

181. The clause introduced by *se* has an unusual aspect in that, although it appears conditional, it merely introduces an exclamation akin to *se Diex m'aïst* (see n. 204) attesting to the truth of the affirmation in vs 182: 'by the joy I have of you!'

182. The illogical repetition of *que* after the intervention of a conditional or a relative clause is attested in the earliest Old French texts and its use increases in frequency throughout the medieval period. See the detailed treatment of "*que* pléonastique" in Graeme-Ritchie, pp. 169-75 and the examples given by Foulet, *Syntaxe*, § 494.

186. The variant *Si en estoie* seems preferable in that, instead of a full stop after vs 185, *Si* would follow logically from *Mais*, and vs 187 would serve to conclude the couplet: 'But I was afraid it was someone else and so was greatly frightened; you must not be surprised at this.' But the reading of *D* is acceptable as a subordinate clause: 'But I was afraid it was someone else; if I was greatly frightened, you ought not be surprised.' This latter expression is a veritable cliché in Old French. Wagner, pp. 463, 467, 471, lists examples of the type "*se + imperf. indic. . . .pres. indic*" from the *Gormont et Isembart* and the *Mort Artu*, and numerous occurrences are found in the works of Rutebeuf (Bastin-Faral, I, 185) and the *Huon de Bordeaux*, p. 39.

204. *se Diex m'aïst:* on the substitution of the conjunction *se* for the adverb *si* and the resultant change to subject-verb order (cf. *Si m'aïst Diex* 170), see Lucien Foulet, "*Si m'aït Dieus* et l'ordre des mots," *Romania*, 53 (1927), 301-24. He makes the interesting point that, with the replacement of *si m'aït Dieus* by *se Dieus m'aït*, an expression of direct Latin origin with a popular ring, the older expression was ousted by a locution which is "avant tout littéraire" (p. 310). See the remarks by Jensen, pp. 18-19, and Orr, p. 19. Duncan McMillan, *Charroi*, n. 382, notes that, in spite of its aspect as a hypothetical clause, *se Diex m'aïst* remains merely an exclamation expressing a guarantee of the truth stated in the main clause and that it is equivalent to English "so help me God!" He explains the form of the present subjunctive *aï*st (< *ait*) either as an influence from the imperfect subjunctive, as an inverse spelling produced by the fall of *s* before an unvoiced consonant, or as an attempt to differentiate it from *ait* < HABEAT. On the possibility that the *s* is phonetic, see la Chaussée, p. 190. On the whole question, see Robert de Dardel, "La forme de la conjonction latine *si* en roman," *Zeitschrift für romanische*

Philologie 94 (1978), 257-66, esp. pp. 263-64, and "Les propositions optatives romanes introduites par *si* et *se*," *Neophilologus* 62 (1978), 39-50, where he argues that, instead of a replacement of the adverb by the conjunction, both types of optative clauses were possible in proto-Romance.

206. On the pleonastic use of *il*, see Nyrop, V, 260: "Le pronom relatif était autrefois repris à l'aide d'un pronom personnel, surtout dans les cas où les deux verbes se suivaient à quelque distance," but the earliest example he gives is from Malherbe. This usage was however well known in Old French: *Qui vos pendroit a vostre corde. . ., Il avroit fet bone jornee* (Rutebeuf; Bastin-Faral, II, vss 246-48) and in Old Provençal: *Lo duc tos paire, el mi donec Monclar (Daurel et Beton*, ed. Paul Meyer, vs 1652).

213. *lui*: not an unusual feminine tonic pronoun for the period (Gossen, *Grammaire*, §65, Foulet, *Syntaxe*, §154, and Sneyders de Vogel, §70). The correction seemed advisable however since it is an isolated example in the *Braies*.

220. *pris' a l'ain*: 'caught on a hook,' whence 'be in difficult straits.' I have not found this expession elsewhere with the meaning it has here. *Prendre a l'ain (ameçon)* is a fishing metaphor commonly employed with the meaning 'to be caught in Satan's snare,' or 'to be snatched away by death:' *quant la mors l'ot pris a l'ain (Mahomet*, 316); but its most common occurrence is a courtly expression 'to be caught on Love's hook, to be overwhelmed by love' (*T.-L*, I, 239). Cf. the *Poire*:

>   Des lors fu pris a l'ameçon.   1820
>   Et qui fu l'aim? Vostre façon

It is noteworthy that Andreas derives, in the manner of Isidore of Seville (*Etymologies*, X, i. 5), AMOR from HAMUS (Book I, Ch. 3).

223. *robe* here designates a complete set of outer clothing (see n. 307 and Reid, p. 112, n. 82).

226. *deliees* (< DELICATAS), an adjective commonly applied in Old French to fine or costly cloth, is found frequently in the works of Chrétien de Troyes (*Yvain*, 2975; *Perceval*, 3355; *Erec*, 404; *Cligés*, 1147). The rhyme *bailliees: deliees* is of course the diphthong -*ie*

with the *i* of *deliees* serving as both the vowel *i* and the yod element of the diphthong (see also vss 319-20). Tobler, *Versbau*, p. 137, furnishes examples of this rhyme for post-medieval poetry. According to Ruelle, *Congés*, p. 44, "...il s'agit partout d'une rime en *-ier* monosyllabique [*i e*] rendue possible par la double valeur de voyelle et de semi-voyelle que possède dans la deuxième série l'élément *i* (prononcé [*i i*])."

238. *savoir de Renart*: a common expression meaning 'to be sly, devious.' The *T.-L.*, V, 771, interprets *Renart* as a common noun "Fuchs," but here it is evident that *savoir de Renart* is a reference to the famous fox, Cf. *Courtois d'Arras*:

> plus set Porrete de Renart   358
> que vous ne savés d'Insangrin.

240. The hypometric verse is easily rectified by the addition of *il* authorized by *A*. Although I have found no other example of *grant eure et grant jorz*, it is to be preferred to the reading of *A*. The *T.-L.*, VI, 1211, registers only *grant eure de jors* from the *MR* text of the *Braies* with the meaning "späte Tagesstunde," but, noticing that *jors* was in the wrong case, suggested the correction "(1. jor: tor)." But since *torz* (ms *A*) is certainly genuine (both manuscripts give the oblique plural *toz*), we should doubtless consider the *A* reading corrupt (and delete it from the *T.-L.*), and *jorz*, nominative singular, a reflection of the exemplar. The only difficulty remaining is the nominative singular masculine *grant*, in all probability a repetition of the feminine in the same verse.

256. *quant*: a subordinate conjunction with the force of 'if;' see the discussion by Imbs, pp. 90-94: "...il est une troisième série de cas où, incontestablement, la valeur conditionnelle de *quant* est au premier plan et étouffe presque totalement la valeur temporelle primitive" (p. 92). Contrary to Lerch, pp. 306-08, vss 255-56 represent a good example of a hypothetical sentence constructed on the model *Quant + cond....cond*: 'I would conceive a child if I had the breeches....' The earliest example of this construction in Wagner, p. 475, seems to be from the *Mémoires* of Commines, although the model *Se + cond... cond.* was current in Old French.

265. *a geün*: an adverbial expression with the meaning 'on an empty

stomach.' Cf. the same rhyme *a jeün: Meün* in the *Roman de la Rose* (10567-68).

270. Rather than "prix d'un repas" as Nardin, p. 50, interpreted *escot* from the *Braies*, it should be glossed literally in keeping with its etymon, Frankish **skot* 'contribution,' specifically, according to Félix Lecoy, "Notes sur le *Testament* de Villon," *Romania* 80 (1959), 513, the "part que l'on doit payer à l'occasion d'une dépense faite en commun." This is precisely the situation here: the merchant, having eaten with the others, was to pay his share (*son escot*) of the bill (see *T.-L.*, III, 982-83). Scott correctly translates: "Quand il vint à payer sa part" (p. 94).

279. It is difficult to determine whether the couplet 279-80 is genuine or an addition by the *D* scribe. It is possible to argue that he omitted the object of *apele*, and so added *sa feme* in the following verse, filling out the couplet with material of his own invention. On the other hand, the antecedent of *l'* in *A* is not expressed in what immediately precedes, and the presence of witnesses to the husband's shame does mark once again the author's insistence on the truth of his tale by repeating the allusion to eye witnesses at the market.

282. While the reading *conclus* 'vanquished, beaten, confounded' (*T.-L.*, II, 656) is perfectly acceptable, the variant *confus* 'shamed' (*T.-L.*, II, 687) does seem the more appropriate in the context for one who has just been publicly humiliated. Cf. the clear example of this meaning in the *T.-L.*: *cele rougi si fu confuse*.

288. *Enpirië avez vostre plet*, 'you have destroyed your case.' Although this is a legal term, it has here overtones of a commercial expression meaning 'lose the deal.' See the examples under *Handel* in the *T.-L.*, IV, 1071-72 and Tilander, pp. 124-25.

299. Again it is difficult to determine whether the couplet is genuine. Note however that the repetition of *Ne* and *de riens* does look suspicious, especially since the scribe was prone to errors of dittography at the beginning of verses (see n. 125).

304. Not only is the *A* reading preferable, but the rich rhyme produced by a verb and its derivative is in the manner of the author.

305. I have emended in accordance with the *A* reading. Not only does the entire couplet 304-05 show signs of corruption, but *De son dos* strikes me as inappropriate in reference to removing one's breeches.

307. '...and lifts up the flaps of his garment.' *Robe* is a general term for clothing applicable to the dress of both men and women (Foulet, *Glossaire*, pp. 261-62). Here it refers to the outer garment worn by the merchant over his breeches, hence the necessity of raising it in order to attach the clerk's breeches to his belt in order to conceal them. Foulet, *Glossaire*, p. 214, defines *pan* as a "large morceau de l'étoffe dont est fait un vêtement," and the *FEW*, VII, 555b, "partie tombante d'une certaine ampleur." It is clear from the examples in the *T.-L.*, VII, 116-18, that the *robe* was made of two wide pieces of fabric draped over the shoulders and sewn along the sides and in back and front.

313. The conjunction *jusqu'atant que*, rare in Old French according to Ménard, p. 220, governs either the indicative or the subjunctive, although in the case of the former the tense is most often the future or the conditional (Jensen, p. 77). But see the *T.-L.*, IV, 1898-99, where several examples are given which, as here, are followed by the preterite.

318. Strictly speaking this is not a correction since, for the scribe, the fall of *l* + consonant caused *si* and *cil* to become homophonous. The deletion of *li* follows *A* and was made because the Friar had not yet appeared.

320. *deslïer* has, to be sure, its literal meaning 'to free, liberate, exonerate,' 'to extricate,' but it is also possible to hear an echo of confessional vocabulary 'to absolve' (as indeed also *regehir* 'to confess' in vs 243). See Matt. 16:19: "...et quodcumque ligaveris super terram erit ligatum in caelis, et quodcumque solveris super terram erit solutum in caelis" (cf. also Matt. 18:18), translated in the *Evangiles des Domnèes:...et quanque tu lïeras sus terre sera lïë es cielz, et quanque tu deslïeras en terre sera deslïë es cielz* (p.156). Cf. *T.-L.*, II, 1634. The use of such precise sacramental vocabulary might be seen in the light of the contemporary struggle of the Mendicant orders with the secular clergy over the power of the confessional (see Introduction, p. 5).

325. As often in Old French *conseillier* means 'to whisper,' not 'to express privately.' Cf. a passage from the *Erec*, with the same rhyme as here, which the *T.-L.*, II, 727, recorded under "vertraulich reden:"

>   Arrieres se tret et consoille
>   A un des vaslez an l'oroille   4090

but which Foerster-Breuer correctly gloss "raunen," and another from the *Ami et Amile* (345) which the editor also glosses "chuchoter."

335. *que*, 'in such a manner that, so that.' Cf. Ménard, § 248.

344. Cf. the same rhyme *marie: Marie* in the *Violette* (6644). This play on words was a literary commonplace often associated with the *planctus* of the Virgin: *Marrie et non Marie* (Grace Frank, ed., *Passion d'Autun*, n. 738).

347. None of the meanings given by Godefroy, X, 703b, and the *T.-L.*, IX, 954-55, for *soupeçon*, 'suspicion, fear, doubt, apprehension,' seems to fit exactly the context for *estre en soupeçon de*, since it is not suspicion or fear of jealousy that the husband promises to forgo forever, but the feeling, occasion of jealousy. We should understand then: 'where you are concerned I shall never again be subject to jealousy.'

350. Rather than a causal conjunction (and the causal link is very weak indeed), *que* could well function as a relative subject pronoun with *La dame* (348) as antecedent (see n. 3).

353. *beçaces*, a sack for provisions made in two parts with a single opening to be carried over the shoulder (Cf. the *FEW* and Du Cange, s.v. BISACCIA). The expression *sac a beçaces* seems curiously redundant. I have not found elsewhere the expression *tendre (rendre) le sac a beçaces a qq.*, though the context clearly suggests the meaning 'to deceive, to put it over on someone.' The *T.-L*, I, 936, lists only this example of the expression and qualifies it as *sprichwörtlich;* however, none of the collections of medieval proverbs has yielded a second example.

358. The reflexive *soi chevir*, synonymous with *venir a chief* (235), means 'to succeed in one's plans.' Cf. *Baillet* (Johnson-Owen, pp. 28-33);

> Qu'ele s'acointa d'un prestre joli,
> Mes le çavatier molt bien s'en chevi. 8

See Foulet, *Glossaire*, p. 42: "se tirer d'affaire" and the *T.-L.*, II, 375, "sich durchbringen, sich heraushelfen."

Index of Proper Names

Amors 18 *personification*, god of love
cordelier 314, 319 Minorite, Franciscan Friar (*s* **frere menor**)
deables 116* demons, devils
Dieu 146, 195, 216, 247, **Diex** *nom* 112, 170, 204*, 328, 336
flabel 360, **fablel** *A* fabliau
frere menor 242, 257, **frere menuz** 339 Minorite, Franciscan Friar (*s* **cordelier**)
Jesucrist 64, **Jhesucrist** 245
maufe *A* devil 116
Meün 57, 96, 266, **Meün sor Loire** 33 Meung-sur-Loire
Orliens 3 Orleans
Renart 238* Renard the Fox
saint Gile 152* Saint Giles
saint Richier 107 Saint-Riquier
seinte Croiz 170* Holy Cross
sainte Marie 135, 344*
toz Sainz 94 All Saints

Glossary

With the exception of some common pronouns, prepositions, conjunctions, relatives, demonstratives, and possessives employed in usual syntactic constructions, the glossary includes all words and their first four occurrences in the text. The forms of nouns and adjectives are those of the oblique singular, when present. Verb forms are grouped under the infinitive, even if it does not appear in the text, and the persons are numbered 1 to 6. Past participles are admitted with the verb except when they are isolated and function solely as adjectives. An asterisk following a number refers to a note to the text, and *A* indicates that the word is found only in manuscript *A*.

a *prep* 153, 350 with; **a la parole** 176 by your voice
aaisier *A s* aisier
acoler *tr* embrace; *pr 3* acole 179, 341; *pp* acolez 74
adonques *adv* 75 then
afaire *m* trade; *adv expression* en son afaire 158 on business
afiner *tr* end, conclude; *pp* afiné 359
aguet *m* 9 ruse; *adv expression* en aguet 46 mindful, watchful
aidier *tr* help; *pr subj 3* aïst 170, 204*, 246, 328; *interj* aïe 135
aim *s* amer
ain *m* 220* fish hook
ainsi *adv* 259 thus
ainz *conj* 219, 232 rather; **ainz que** *subor conj* 96 before
aisie aaisie, *A adj;* **estre bien aisie de** 348 be quite free to
aïst *s* aidier
ajornee *A f* 43 daybreak
aler *intr* 33, 92, 355 go; **s'en aler** 205, 207 depart; *pr 1* vois 108; *3* vait 77, 85, 125, 287; vet 45, 262; *5* alez 152, 159; *pf 3* ala 91, 269; *pp* alez 73, 110
aloigne *f* postponement; **faire d'aloigne** 78 draw out
ame *f* 114 soul
amen *excl* 338 so be it!
amende *f* 345 amends
amer *tr* 11 love, be fond of; *pr 1* aim 171; *3* aime 206; *impf 3* amoit 7, 31; *pf 3* ama 20, 87
amie *f* 145, 204 beloved
amis *m* 113, 210 love, lover
amor *f* 206, 350 love; **amors** 11*, 227
an *s* en

ançois *adv* 173 sooner, first
antre *prep* 22 between
apareillier *tr* ready, prepare; *pf 3* apareilla 193; *pp* apareilliez 40
apeler *tr* 91 call; *pr 3* apele 111, 278; *pf 3* apela 124, 127
aporter *tr* bring; *pr 1* aport 332
après *prep* 27 after
aprise *adj* 17 learned
argent *m* 271 money
arrieres arriers, *adv* 167, 262 back
asené *adj*; estre mal asené 115* be in a sorry state
assenbler *intr* come together; *pp* assenblé 214
assez *adv* 309 a great deal
atant *adv* 66, 109, 237, 262 then, thereupon; 360 now; *subor conj* jusqu'atant que 313* until
atargier A *m* 28 delay
atendre *tr* 71 wait
atorner *tr* make ready; *pp* atornez 59
aucun *indef pron* 280 some persons
aumoire *f* 334 wardrobe
ausi *s* come
autre *pron* 185 another; autres 98 the other; 267, 269 the others; *adj* autres 217, 315 other
aval *adv* 312 down, through
avenir *intr* occur, happen; *pf 3* avint 3*, 6, 283; *pp* avenue 198
aventure *f* 2 story, tale; mal' aventure 309 misfortune
avertiz *adj* 41* instructed, forewarned
avis *m* opinion; ce m'est avis 211, 231 it seems to me
avoir *tr* 24, 336 have; *pr 1* ai 52, 169, 174, 251; *3* A 69, 112, 121, 149; *4* avons 53, 94; *5* avez 55, 90, 137, 150 (*s* que); *6* ront 116 (*s* ramener); *pf 3* ot 18, 70, 76, 190; *6* orent 123, 215; *impf 1* avoie 185, 254; *3* avoit 26, 34, 67; *fut 3* avra 141; *cond 1* avroie 256; *pr subj 1* aie 181; *5* aiez 297; *imper 5* aiez 292

baillier *tr* give; *pp* bailliees 225
baisier *tr* kiss; *pr 3* baise 212, 341; *pp* baisiez 75
beau *adj* 23, 51, 179 fine; beax 93, 102, 113, 210; bele 145, 204; *with noun, term of endearment* (*s* sire, conpainz, amis, amie); estre beles a 316 like, please

beçaces *f* 353* double sack
besoig *m* 67* need, desire
besoigne *f* 77 affair, business
bien *adv* 14, 235 indeed; 17, 19, 39, 40 well; 97, 100, 348 very
blanches *A adj* 226 white
blasmer *tr* blame, accuse; *pp* blasmee 298
bon *adj* 261 good (*s* gre); bones 226
bordel *m* 155 whorehouse
borgois borjois, *m* 45, 58, 66, 76 townsman, merchant
borjoise borgoise, *f* 7, 16, 35, 61 townswoman, merchant's wife
borse *f* 277 purse
bouche *f* 212 mouth
bouter *tr* throw; *pp* boutees 252; *refl* jump into bed; *pr 3* boute 178
braier *m* 229 belt, waist
braies *f* 122, 200, 217, 219 breeches
braz *m* 22, 86 arms
brisier *tr* 117 break
bruit *m* 153 clamor, noise

caienz *adv* 155 herein
celer *tr* 206 hide, conceal
certainement *adv* 54 assuredly
certes *adv* 52, 164, 177 indeed
chacier *A tr* 241 drive away
chanbre *f* 301 bedchamber
changier *tr* 241 convert
chaucier *tr* put on one's breeches; *pr 3* chauce 305
chevir *refl* get out of a difficulty; *fut 3* chevira *A* 234; *pp* chevie 358*
chief *m* 286 head; venir a chief 235 arrange a successful outcome
chiere *adj* 145 dear
chose *f* 297 thing, object
ci *adv* 112, 138, 333 here
cité *f* 3 town
clerc *m* 20, 24, 38, 88; clers 7, 69, 74, 80 clerk, student
coiement *adv* 326 softly, quietly
coite *f* 252 mattress, quilt
col *m* 117 neck

commander *tr* entrust, commend, bid; *pr 1* **commant** 64; *3* **commande** 227; *pf 3* **commanda** 37, 195

come, comme, con *conj* 18, 41*, 268 as, as befits; 128, 169, 308 like; **si con, si comme** 6, 72, 90 as; **ausi con se** 133 just as if; **tantost con** 317 as soon as; *excl* 112 what

commancier *tr* begin; *pr 3* **commance** 323

comment *inter adv* 247, 287 how

concevoir *tr* 253 conceive a child; *cond 1* **concevroie** 255; *pp* **conceü** 337

conclus *adj* 282* confounded

confus A *adj* 282* shamed

congié *m* 338 leave

connoistre *tr* recognize; *pr 1* **connois** 176; *impf 1* **connoissoie** 182; *pf 1* **connui** 173; *impf subj 1* **conneüsse** 183

conpainz *m* 93, 99, 102, 105 companion

conplot *m* 87* tussle

conseiller *tr* whisper; *pr 3* **conseille** 325*

conte *m* 322 tale, account

contenance *f* face; **faire liee contenance** 81* exhibit a joyful expression

conter *tr* tell; *pr 1* **conte,** 16

convoier *tr* lead, accompany, *pr 3* **convoie** 61

coraige *m* 26* intention; 190 desire

cordelier *m* 314, 319 Franciscan (*s* Index of Proper Names)

cors *paraphrastic pron* 65 yourself; 103 myself

cortoise *adj* 8 elegant, of genteel manner

cosche *s* couchier

couche *f* 86* bed

couchier *refl* 45, 108, 125 go to bed; *pr 3* **couche** 85, **cosche** 129; *pf 1* **couchai,** 168; *pp* **couchiez** 139, 148

couvenir *impers intr* be necessary, must; *pr 3* **couvient** 12, **covient** 14, 205; *impf 3* **covenoit** 32

covrir *tr* 15 conceal; *refl* protect; *fut 3* **couverra** 234

cox *m* 357 cuckold

crïer *intr* cry out; *fut 1* **crïerai** 153

cuer *m* 52, 292, 329 heart

cuidier *tr* think, believe; *pr 5* **cuidiez** 161; *pf 3* **cuida** 271

cure *f* 1 care (*s* mestre)

dame *f* 46, 113, 126, 157 lady; 162, 247, 260, 286 term of address

dangier *A m* 230 resistence
delai *m* 83 delay (*s* n. 82)
delaier *A intr* 314 delay
delez *prep* 129, 168, 178 beside
deliees *adj* 226* delicate, fine
delit *m* 24, 140 pleasure, sexual favors
demeure *f* 55 delay
demorance *f* 82* delay
demoree *f* 44* delay
derechief *adv* 236 once again
descoschier *refl* rise from bed; *pp* **descoschié** 58
descouvenue *f* 197 misfortune, disaster
desennor *f* 196 shame, dishonor
deslïer *tr* 320* absolve, exonerate
desmentir *tr* deny, contradict; *pp* **desmenti** 149
desoz *prep* 252 beneath
despendre *tr* spend; *pp* **despendu,** 351
desplaire *intr* displease; *pr subj 3* **desplaise,** 162, 300, 342
despoillier *m* 83 act of undressing (*s* n. 82)
devant *prep* 43 before (*temp*)
devoir *tr* must, owe; *pr 1* **doi** 298, 344; *3* **doit** 206; *5* **devez** 187; *impf 3* **devoit** 92, 320 was to
dire *tr* 6, 132 say, tell, speak; *pr 1* **di** 79, 107; *3* **dit** 113; *5* **dites,** 106, 210; *pf 3* **dist,** 27, 63, 93, 106, **dit,** 218; *cond 1* **diroie,** 281; *pr subj 1* **die,** 264; *3* **die** 228; *imper* **dites** 248, 286 *A*, 259; *pp* **dit** 138, 203, 232, 286
dit *A m* 2 tale
dolente *A adj* 222 grieved
donc *adv* 108 then, therefore
doner *tr* give; *pf 3* **dona** 5; *pr subj 3* **doint** 336
dont *rel pron* 123 as a result of which; 322 about which
dormir *intr* sleep; *pf 3* **dormi** 49, 191; *imper* **dormez** 189; *pp* **dormi** 54, 70, 94
dos *m* 223 back
doucement *adv* 232 softly, gently
douter *tr* fear; *pr 3* **doute** 233
douz *adj* 113, **douce** 145 dear, sweet (*term of endearment*)
el[1] *contr* en le 329
el[2] *pers pron* 14, 30, 127, 133 she
en *adv pron* 5 of it; 80, 174, 175, 177 in this matter; 149 9, 190 it; 233, 356 about it; 42, 159, **an** 152 away (*with vb of motion*)

encor *adv* 104 yet
endormi *m* sleeping person; **faire l'endormi** 126* pretend to be asleep
endormie *adj* 30 asleep
enfant *m* 256 child
engigneuse *adj* 239 clever, cunning
enging *m* 9, 13 deceit
enjornee *f* 43 daybreak
enlacier *tr* ensnare; *pp* **enlaciee** 19
ennoïer *tr* bother, vex; *pr subj 3* **ennuit** 166
enpirier *tr* ruin, endanger, spoil; *pp* **enpirié** 288*
enprunter *tr* borrow; *pp* **enpruntees** 251
ensaignier *tr* indicate; *impf subj 3* **ensaignast** 319
entendre *tr* 72 understand
entente *f* 1 attention, effort (*s* mestre)
entor *prep* 305 around, off
entrebaisier *refl* kiss one another; *pr 6* **entrebaisent**, 236
entrecommander *refl* commend one another; *pr 6* **entrecommandent** 216
entrefaire *refl* do to one another, perform together, *pr 6* **entrefont** 213
entrer *intr* 41 enter; *pf 3* **entra** 317; *pp* **entrez** 125
enui *m* 174 trouble, distress; **enuiz** 103 harm
ere erent, *s* estre
errer *intr* 67, 101 set out, travel
esbahir *refl* be dumbfounded, astonished, *pr 1* **esbahis** 172, 177; *pf 3* **esbahist** 105; *pp* **esbahiz** 282; **esbahie** 222, 290
escot *m* 270* share of the bill
escrïer *refl* cry out; *pp* **escrïee** 134
escritoire *f* 273 writing case, pouch
esfroi *A* 142 fright
esjoïr *refl* rejoice; *pf 3* **esjoï** 35; *pp* **esjoï** 263
esmoi *m* fright; **estre en esmoi que** 142 be fearful, worried lest
espox *m* 147 husband
estovoir *impers intr* be necessary, obliged; *fut 3* **estovra**, *A* 356
estre *intr* 298 be; *pr 1* **sui**, 136, 147, 167; *3* **est**, 58, 60, 109, 110; *4* **somes** 115; *5* **estes** 99, 100, 160, 163; *6* **sont** 214, 218, 219, 226; *impf 1* **estoie** 148, 186; *3* **estoit** 8, **ere** 274; *6* **erent** 314; *pf 3* **fu** 17, 46, 59, 68; *6* **furent** 280; *pr subj 3* **soit** 65; *impf subj 1* **fusse** 184; *3* **fust** 30, 39, 40, 133; *fut 1* **serai** 346;

3 sera, 97, 296; *6* seront 316; *imper* soiez 299; *pp* esté 76
esveillier *tr* 48 awake; *impf subj 3* esveillast 29; *refl* awaken; *pf 3* esveilla 50
esveilliez *adj* 39 alert
eure *f* 101 hour; a eure 56 on time; grant eure 240* late in the day

fablel *A m* 360 fabliau
faire *tr* 157, 161, 349 do, make, cause, say; *pr 3* fait 10, 105, 108, 126; fet 169; *fut 1* ferai 260, 345; *5* feroiz 189; *cond 1* feroie 44, 78; *pf 1* fis 171; *3* fist 88, 127, 312, 338; *6* firent 81, 82; *pp* fait 55, 174, 215; fet 169; faite 343; **faire que** + *adj* 189 behave; **faire** + *masc noun* 126*, 127, 130, 156 pretend, act like (*s* n. 126); **faire mauvaise** 161 debase, debauch; **faire demeure, demoree, demorance,** 44*, 55, 82 linger, delay; **faire d'aloigne** 78 prolong (*s* n. 44); **faire liee contenance** 81* put on a happy face, countenance; **faire enui, marie** 174, 343 distress, **faire lor geu** 215 copulate; *verbum vicarium* 169, 171
farouche *m* 130 fright (*s* faire)
feme *f* 10, 163 woman; 26, 143, 279, 285 wife
fille *f* 253 daughter
filz *m* 253 son
finer *tr* terminate, end: *pr 3* fine 118, 360 *A*; pp finé 360
flabel *m* 360 fabliau
foi *f* 344 faith
foire *f* 34 market, fair
foiz *f* 169 times, occasions
forment *adv* 36 greatly
fors *prep* 122, 141 except
forsaner *intr* go mad; *pr 3* forsanne 276; *pp* forsenee 133; forsenez 99
fox *adj* 95, 160 fole 175 mad
freor *f* 186 terror

garantir *refl* 13 protect oneself
garde *f* 65 protector, gardien
garder *tr* protect; *pr subj 3* gart 103
garnemenz *m* 228 equipment, objects
gent *f* 272 people
gesir *intr* lie, sleep with; *pf 6* jurent 86; *impf subj 3* geüst 22

geu, gieu *m* 214, 215 game, sport
geün *adj* fasting; **a geün** 265* hungry
gié *tonic pers pron* 260 I
grant *adj m* 47, 83, 174, 190, *f* 52, 55, 82, 123 much, great, (*s* **eure**)
gre *m* will; **de bon gre** 261 willingly
guenges *f* 12* tricks

hardie *adj* 289 bold
hardiement *adv* 291 boldly
haucier *tr* raise; *pr 3* **hauce**, 306
haute *adj* 134 high, loud
hennor *m* 241 honor
hom *m* 140 man (*s* **nus**)
honte *f* 15, 241, 321 shame, disgrace
hors *adv* 66, 151, 160, 209 out
hort *m* 128 deceit, deception
hui *adv* 57 today
huschier *intr* 118 cry out

i *adv* 121, 125 there; 154 here
iluec, ilueques *adv* 68, 109, 237 there
ire *f* 52, 123 sorrow, vexation; 180, 292 anger
isnelepas *adv* 202 quickly
issir[1] *intr* 209 leave, go out, depart; *pf 3* **ist** 66; *impf subj 3* **issist** 143 (*s* **sens**); *pp* **issue** 184, 224
issir[2] *m* 63 departure

ja *adv* 153 immediately; **ja. . .ne** 140, 181, 184, 346 never (*s* **mais**)
jalousie *f* 347* jealousy
joie *f* 181, 329 joy, delight; **a joie** 336 joyously
joieuse *A adj* 181 joyful
jor *m* 32, 198, 284 day; **grant jorz** 240* late in the day; **point du jor** 28, 191 daybreak; **jor de sa vie** 357 as long as he lives
jurent *s* **gesir**
jusque *prep* 62 up to; 191 until; *conj* 313 until (*s* **atant**)

la *adv* 314 there
laienz *adv* 42, 63, 317 inside
laz *m* 19 trap, snares
lessier *A tr* refrain from; *impf subj 3* **lessast** 29
leus *m* 354 places
lever *tr* raise; *pr 3* **lieve** 307; *intr* 32 get up, rise from bed; *imper* **levez** 119; *pp* **levez** 89, 164*, 323
lez *prep* 148 alongside
liee *adj* 81* happy, joyful
lit *m* 23, 132, 139, 184 bed
lober *tr* trick, beguile; *pr 3* **lobe** 308
loiax *adj* 147 legal, lawful
loig *adv* 68 far, distant (see n. 67)
longue *A adj* 78 prolongued, drawnout
longuement *adv* 53, 231 for a long time
lordel *adj* 156* foolish, stupid (*s* **putain**)
lors *adv* 58, 68, 74, 111 then

mainte *adj* 169, 272 many
maintenant *adv* 38 quickly; 120, 178, 306 immediately
mais *conj* 45*, 79 now; 185, 196 but; 300 rather; *adv* 56, 57 yet; 171 ever before; 355 henceforth; **ja mais** 346, 357 never more
maison *f* 209 house
mal *adv* 115* badly (*s* **asené**)
malaise *f*; **en malaise** 299 upset
malbaillie *adj* 136 undone, destroyed
male *adj* 112; **mal'**, 309 bad (*s* **aventure**)
malement *adv* 222 greatly
mander *tr* send word, announce; *pf 3* **manda** 38
marcheanz *m* 268 merchant
marchié *m* 34, 57, 266 market
marir *refl* be upset, angry; *imper* **marisiez** 146; *pp* **marie** 343*
matin *m* 192 morning; *adv* 207 early
matire *f* 5 subject matter
mauvaise *adj* 161 debauched (*s* **faire**); **mauvese** 250 wicked (*s* **tenir**)
meïsme *adj* 284 same, very
mengier[1] *tr* 269 eat
mengier[2] *m* 27 evening meal
menor *s* **frere menor** *in Index of Proper Names*

mentir *intr* 14 lie; *pp* menti 150
menuz *s* frere menor *in Index of Proper Names*
merci *m* 137 pity, mercy
merveillier *refl* 187 wonder, marvel
mesprendre *intr* be mistaken; *pp* mespris 199
mestier *m* 17 affair; faire tel mestier 10 engage in such business; avoir mestier de 188 need
mestre *tr* 1 put, place; *pp* mis 351; mise 18, 329; mises 334
midi *m* 97 midday
mie *adv* 29, 100, 146, 155 in any way, at all
mielz *adv* 171 better
mïenuit *f* 165; mïenuiz 104 midnight
moillier *f* 84 wife
molt *adv* 8, 9, 52, 81 very; 128, 238 very much; 20, 21, 35 greatly
mostier *m* 313 monastery
mot *m* word; sanz dire mot 132 without saying anything

nouvele *f* 112; noveles 315 news
nuit *f* night; la nuit 39 that night; de tote la nuit 71 all night long; cele nuit 255 this past night
nului *indef pron* 318 anyone
nus *adj*; nus hom 140 no man
nuz *adj* 22, 84, 168 naked

o *prep* 23, 84, 267, 269 with
oblïer *tr* forget, neglect; *pf 3* oublia 122; *impf subj 3* obliast 29
ocire *tr* kill; *pp* ocise 330
oïr *tr* hear; *fut 3* orra 315; *pf 1* oï 6; *3* oï 36; *pr subj 3* oie 335; *pp* oï 90, 244, 322; oïe 221
onques *adv* 171 ever; ne...onques 70, 76 never
or *adv* 51, 77, 93, 119 now (*s* sus); ore 15*, 175 now
oraille *f* 326 ear
orendroit *adv* 205 immediately
oser *tr* dare; *fut 3* osera 356
ostel *m* 60, 110, 285, 340 house, dwelling
ovuec ovueques *prep* 92, 301 with

païer *tr* 270 pay

pans *m* 307* hems, folds, flaps
paor *f* 185 fear
par *prep* 94, 107, 114, 152 by; 331 through; 276, 330 (*s* **poi**); 315 (*s* **tans**)
parchemin *m* 275 parchment
pardoner *tr* forgive; *imper* **pardonez** 180
parler *intr* 356 speak
parole *f* 36, 221 words; 176 voice
part *f* 324 side, aside
partir *intr* leave; *pr 3* **part**, 237; *pp* **partiz** 42
pas *adv* 68, 104, 165, 182 not
passer *tr* cross; *pp* **passé** 69
pechié *m* 331 fault
peine *f*; a peine 56 scarcely
pendre *tr* hang, suspend; *impf 6* **pendoient** 229; *pp* **pendues** 311
penne *f* 275 quill, pen
peser *impers* grieve, distress; *pr 3* **poise** 80
pesme *A adj* 112 terrible
place *f* 354 place; estre en la place 280 be present
plaire *impers* please; *pf 3* **plot** 88; *impf subj 3* **pleüst**, 21
plenté *f* abundance; a grant plenté 350 in great quantity
plet *m* 288* case; **plait**, 359 affair
plus *adv* 74, 78, 165, 188 more, longer; **au plus soef que** 144* as softly as; **sanz plus** 28, 62 without further ado
poi *m* 343 little; **par poi...ne** 276, 330 almost
point *m* 28, 191 (*s* **jor**); *adv* 80 not at all
poise *s* peser
pooir *intr* can, be able; *pr 4* **poons** 95; 5 **poez**, 72; *fut 3* **porra** 355; *pf 3* **pot** 144; *pr subj 4* **puission** 96; *6* **puissent** 117
por *prep* 71, 241, 253 in order to; 131, 175, 350 for; **por Dieu** 146, 180, 247 for God's sake; **por Jhesucrist** 245 for Christ's sake; **por ce** 207 for this reason
porpens *m*; estre en porpens de 47* be mindful, alert to
porter *tr* 312 bring, carry; *pp* **portees** *A* 251
pranre *tr* 271 take; *pf 3* **prist** 121, 217, 338; *pp* **pris** 200, **pris'** 220*, **prises** 333
premerain *adj* 48 first (*s* **some**)
pres *prep* 97 near
preu *m* 31* advantage
preude *adj* 163 good, worthy

preudom', prodome *m* 47, 91 good, worthy man
proier *tr* 230 ask, beg; *pr 1* **pri** 166; *3* **prie** 227, 245
prouver *tr* prove; *pp* **prouvé** 296
provee *adj* 278 proven, notorious
puis *adv* 138, 179, 213, 218 then; 123 afterwards
putain *f* 278 whore; **faire le putain lordel** 156* act like a filthy whore (*s* n. 126)

quanivez *m* 274 pen knife
quanque *indef pron* 121 whatever
quant *conj* 36, 42, 50, 69 when; 256* if
quanz *indef pron* 267 how many
quar *conj* 199, 254 for
quas *m* 283 event
quatre *adj* 75 four
que *conj* 181, 182*, 350*, 356 for, because; 335* so that; *interrog pron* 44, 78 why; **qu'avint** 3* which happened; **que vos avez** 293 what is wrong with you
quel *interrog adj* 26* what
qui *interrog pron* 138, 139 who; *impers pron* 206* he who

raconter *tr* 2 tell, relate
raison *f* reason; **or est raison** 264 now it is fitting; **dire raison** 210 speak wisely
raler *intr* go away; *imper* **ralez** 159
ramener *tr* bring back; **deables le ront amené** 116* demons have brought him back
reconoistre *tr* attest, admit; *pf 6* **reconurent** 279
regehir *tr* confess; *pf 3* **regehi** 243 (*s* n. 320)
remenbrer *impers* relate, recall; *pr 3* **remenbre**, 302
rendre A *tr* return, give back 352 (*s* n. 353)
repondre *refl* hide; *pf 3* **repost** 120
requerre A *tr* beseech; *pr 3* **requiert** 227
respondre *tr* answer; *pf 3* **respondi** 98
retrere *tr* relate, tell; *pp* **retret** 303
revenir *intr* return; *pf 3* **revint** 284
rien *adv* 233, **riens**, 25* nothing; **de riens** 31, 298, 299* in any way
rire *intr* 323 laugh
robe *f* 223*, 307* outer garment

ront *s* avoir *and* ramener
rues *f* 312 streets

sac *m* 353* sack, bag
saige *adj* 8 wise; **faire que saige** 189 act wisely
saillir *intr* leap; *pf 3* sailli 132
saint *m* 107, 152; sainz 94 saint
sainte *adj* 344; seinte 170 holy
sainture *f* 310 waist, belt
sanz *prep* 28, 132, 192 without (*s* plus)
savoir *tr* 12 know; *pr 1* sa 54*; sai 267, 287, 293; *3* set 196, 201, 309; *5* savez 294; *impf 3* savoit 9, 25; *pf 3* sot 128, 157, 238*; *fut 3* savra 235; *pr subj 3* saiche 14; *imper* sachiez 183
se *conj* 137, 167, 181*, 183, 204* if (*s* come)
secourre *tr* help; *pr subj 3* secoure 102
seignor *m* 141, 195, 249; signor 258; sires 25, 37, 43, 50; sire 51, 124, 172, 179 husband; *term of address* 258, 291, 328, 332
sejor *m* delay; **sanz plus de sejor** 192 without further delay
sen *m* 160 mind (*s* sens)
senez *adj* 100 sensible
sens *m* mind; **issir du sens** 143 lose one's mind
seulement *adv* 248 only
si[1] *adv* 6, 72, 90, 271 as; 53, 199 so (*s* come)
si[2] *conj* 166 and
sire sires, *s* seignor
soef *adv* 144* gently, softly (*s* plus)
soir *m* 27 evening
solaz *m* 20, soulaz 140 sexual pleasure
some *m* sleep; **premerain some** 48 first sleep, sleep before midnight
songier *tr* dream; *pp* songié 254, 259, 337
sort *m* deaf person; **faire le sort** 127 pretend to be deaf (*s* n. 126)
sot *m* 131 fool, dolt (*s* tenir)
soupeçon *f* 347* suspicion
sueil *m* 69 threshold
sus *exclam* up; **or sus** 51, 93, 119 get up

tans *m* **par tans** 315 soon
tant *adv* 94, 124 so long
tantost *adv* 317, 324 immediately (*s* come)

tanz *m* 75 times; **quatre tanz baisiez** 75 kissed four times more
targier *intr* 28 linger, delay
tel *adj* 10, 101, 153, 292; **tex** 225 such, such a; **tel ore** 15* time and again
tendre *tr* hold out; *pp* **tendu** 352 (*s* n. 353)
tenir *tr* 95, 131 hold; *pr 1* **tieg** 175; *fut 3* **tendra** 250; **tenir por fox (fole)** 95, 175 consider mad; **tenir por sot** 131 make a fool out of; **tenir por mauvese**, 250 consider dishonored
tesmoigner *tr* affirm, testify; *pr 3* **testmoigne** 4; *6* **tesmoignent** 272
tirer *tr* draw; *pr 3* **tire**, 324
torner *refl* depart, go away; *pp* **tornez**, 109
tors torz *m* deceits, tricks 12*, 239
tost *adv* 59, 119 immediately; 90, 164 early
tot *adv* 38, 326 very; **toz** 22*, 84 completely; *adj* **tuit** 123, 154; **toz** 94, 103, 168, 228; **tote** 71 (*s* **nuit**), 177; **totes** 354 all; *pron* **tot** 244, 303 everything
trahir *tr* betray; *pp* **trahir** 136
trere *tr* take off, remove; *pr 3* **tret** 304*
tres *adv* 145, 197 very
trestot *pron* 325 all, everything
troi *m* 123 three
trop *adv* 30, 55, 90, 164 too
trover *tr* find; *pp* **trové**, 273; **trouvé** 295; **trouvee** 277, 297

ueil *m* eye; **ne dormir de l'ueil** 70 not sleep a wink
uis *m* 62, 111, 114, 124 door, gate

veillier *intr* 188 remain awake; *pf 3* **veilla** 49, 194 be on the watch
venir *intr* 96, 235, 355 come; *pr 3* **vient** 111; *pf 3* **vint** 202, 242, 270, 313; *fut 3* **venra** 249; *5* **venrroiz** 56; *6* **venront** 154; *imper* **venez** 300; *pp* **venuz** 167, 266, 340
veoir *tr* see; *pf 3* **vit** 285; *pr subj 6* **voient** 208; *imper* **vez** 333
verité *f* 4, 294 truth
veroie *adj* true 163
vestir *refl* dress; *pf 3* **vesti** 193; *pp* **vestuz** 59; **vestue** 223
vie *f* 357 life (*s* **jor**)
vilain *m* 131*, 219 fellow, wretch

vile *f* 151 town
vis *m* 212 face
voie *f* 62 road
voir *adv* 106, 107, 254, 296 truly
voisin *m* 154*, 208 neighbors
voiz *f* 134 voice
volenté *f* will; **faire sa volenté** have, take her pleasure 349
volentiers *adv* 261 willingly
voloir *tr* wish, desire; *pr 1* **vueil** 1, 207; *3* **velt** 11; *5* **volez** 101; *impf subj 3* **vosist** 21

Appendices

The basic structure of *Les Braies au cordelier* can be reduced to the following schema: a wife, confronted by a telltale object left by a lover, dupes her husband into believing that the object was not only legitimate, but that its presence proves her virtue and love for him. This is listed in Stith Thompson as motif K1526.[1] To this underlying structure is joined a folk-motif found in tales from Ireland to India and termed by Thompson "magic remedies for barrenness" (T591 in the *Motif-Index*). But these talismanic fertility objects associated with the tale are secondary accretions to its deep structure (what Bédier would call "la forme organique du conte"). This basic story, without the fertility motif, has been traced by numerous scholars (cf. Bédier, p. 451) to a Milesian tale in Chapter IX of Apuleius' *Metamorphoses*. If this tale did migrate to the West, it doubtless constituted the archetype of the numerous analogues found in medieval and renaissance Europe. But the earliest in date seems to have been *Les Braies au cordelier*, followed by *Les Braies le prestre*. A similar story is found in the *Facetiae* of Poggio (No. 231) and in the works of such composers of *novelle* as Sacchetti, Sabadino, Masuccio, Morlino, Sercambi, Boiardo, and others. Since an exhaustive list of the many analogues was drawn up by Johannes Bolte,[2] I shall limit myself here to presenting four of the more interesting and early French analogues: *Les Braies le prestre* by Jean de Condé, an *exemplum* from the *Livre du chevalier de la Tour Landry, La Farce de Frere Guillebert*, and one of the stories from Henri Estienne's *Apologie pour Hérodote*. Finally, an adaptation in prose of *Les Braies au cordelier* by Le Grand d'Aussy is included as an example of eighteenth-century literary interest—a perfect blend of the taste for medieval storytelling with the prudishness of contemporary *bienséance*.

---

[1] *Motif-Index of Folk-Literature*, 6 vols. (Bloomington, 1955).

[2] *Jakob Freys Gartengesellschaft (1556)* (Tübingen, 1896). The note, pp. 248-51, is to Frey's tale *Von sanct Franciscen brůch, wie die uff einner frawen beth funden worden*.

1. Les Braies le Prestre by Jean de Condé

This fabliau of the Hainaut *ménestrel* Jean de Condé († 1346) is preserved in a single manuscript: Rome, Casanatensis 1598 (*olim* Biblioteca della Minerva, B. III. 18), folios 161*d*—162*c*.[1] It has been edited on three previous occasions:

1) Adolf Tobler, *Gedichte von Jehan de Condet nach der casanatensischen Handschrift.* Stuttgart: Bibliothek des litterarischen Vereins LIV, 1860. Pp. 161-164.

2) August Scheler, *Dits et contes de Baudouin de Condé et de son fils Jean de Condé.* 3 vols, Bruxelles: Devaux, 1866-1867. Vol. II, pp. 121-125 (notes pp. 409-10).

3) Anatole de Montaiglon et Gaston Raynaud, *Recueil général et complet des fabliaux des XIIIe et XIVe siècles.* 6 vols, Paris: Librairie des Bibliophiles, 1872-1890. Vol. VI, pp. 257-260.

Apparently only Tobler saw the Rome manuscript; each subsequent editor repeated and added to the errors of his predecessor. Tobler's garbled transcription entailed the loss of three verses; this lacuna was carefully preserved and became the object of speculation by both Scheler and *MR* (see n. 43). The worst text is decidedly that of the *Recueil général* where mistakes in transcription from Scheler's edition are too numerous to record. Indeed, these three editions are little more than extensions of the scribal process, the end result of accumulated error.

I have adhered closely to the single manuscript readings, only

---

[1] On Jean de Condé and his work, see the important thesis of Jacques Ribard, *Un ménestrel du XIVe siècle: Jean de Condé* (Genève, 1969). A description of the Casanatensis manuscript is found in Ernest Langlois, *Notices des manuscrits français et provençaux de Rome antérieurs au XVIe siècle,* in *Notices et extraits des manuscrits de la Bibliothèque Nationale et autres bibliothèques,* XXXII, Pt. 2 (Paris, 1889), 301, and Ribard, pp. 25-26. For a study of the literary superiority of *Les Braies au cordelier* over Jean's fabliau, see Rychner, I, 32-36. English translation by Hellman-O'Gorman, pp. 101-104.

correcting *priestres* in vs 2 to restore the meter and rectifying vs 34 in order to make sense of the scribal corruption. In other respects I follow the editorial procedure adopted for *Les Braies au cordelier*.

161*d*
    Recorder ai oÿ maint conte
Que priestre ont fait as pluisors honte
Et ont a leur femme jeü,
Et avoec çou le leur eü;   4
On en conte maint lait reviel.
S'en dirai un conte nouviel
Qui est estrais de verité.
    Il avoit a unne cité   8
N'a mie lonc tamps un boucier;
Sa femme eut un priestre plus cier
De lui, car mius faisoit sen gre
Quant a li parloit a secré.   12
Li bouciers qui mot n'en savoit
Ens ou markiet aler devoit
O compaingnons de sen mestier;
D'argent çou qu'il en eut mestier   16
Quist pour mouvoir a l'endemain,
Qu'il dist qu'il voloit aler main.
Sa femme fist savoir au priestre
K'en pais poroit avoec lui iestre.   20
Li priestres qui le couvoita
Dou boucier le meute gaita;

162*a*   Celle qui haioit son singnour
Le fist mouvoir devant le jour.   24
Quant de se maison fu issus,
Li priestres qui n'e[s]t mie ensus
S'est ou lit la dame couciés.
    Chius a ses compaingnons huciés;   28
Il dient: "Qui t'a encanté?
Encor n'ont pas li cok canté,
Il est pau plus de mïenuit.
Reva coucier, si ne t'anuit,   32
Car encor pues dormir grant somme;
Il y a en toi songneus homme."
Cieus en revient en sa maison;
Sa femme dist: "Pour quel raison   36

Revenés? Que vous faut il ore?"
—N'en voel[ent] pas aler encore
Li autre," ce dist ses maris.
Li priestres fu tous esmaris; 40
Elle dist que garde n'aroit,
Coi se tenist viers le paroit.
Et li bouciers se recouca,
Mais a sa femme ne touca. 44
Li priestres d'angoisses fremi,
Et li bouciers se rendormi.
Celle fu dou mai[n]s bien partie,
Car dous en eut en sa partie: 48
Li priestres se gisoit a diestre
Et ses maris deviers seniestre.
Et quant vint deviers l'ajourner,
Li autre se vont atourner 52
Et hucierent leur compaingnon.
Si saut sus a loi de gagnon
Et se lieve, plus n'i atent.
As piés de se[n] lit se main tent, 56
Au prendre ses braies mesprent,
Car les braies le priestre prent,
C'onques il ne s'en donna warde.
Haste soi pour çou c'on l'awarde; 60
A ses compaingnons en ala
Et si se parti de dela.
Li priestres remest ens ou lit
Et si demena sen delit; 64
Et quant li plot, si se leva,
Les braies au boucier trouva,
S'i trouva le bourse pesant.
Par lui meïsmes va disant: 68
"Je ne sui pas mout enganés
Quant a l'argent sui assenés;
Boire yrai, point d'argent n'avoie."
Li priestre s'en ala sa voie. 72
Li autre au marciet venut sont,
Biestes pour accater quis ont.
Li bouciers une en acata
Et donné su[r] cel acat a 76
Le denier Dieu sans delaiier,

Puis va a se bourse a braiier,
Qu'il voloit paiier son argent.
Entour lui ot assés de gent. 80
Sa monnoie trouver y cuide,
Mais il trouva sa bourse wide;
Dou priestre y troeve le sayel
Dont fu batus d'un grief flaiiel 84
Et fu de cuer honteus et mas.
"Foy que doi, fait il, saint Thumas,
Ves ci coze trop desghisee!"
Entour lui ot molt grant risee. 88
Li bouciers fu tous entrepris
Et de grant mautalent espris
Quant le saiel au priestre troeve.
Or peut veïr apierte preuve 92
Que li priestres fu de li priés.
Uns siens compains li dist apriés:
"Compains, c'as tu fait de tes braies?
Or as tu ensengnes bien vraies 96
Dou priestre dont le saiel as:
De ta femme fait ses soulas
Et si ert dou tien parçonniers,
Qu'il a te bourse a tes deniers." 100
Li bouciers fut plus abaubis
Qu'entre dis leus une brebis;
162c Et cascuns di[t]: "Vois dou huihot!"
La bieste de quoi paiier n'ot, 104
Trestous desconfis en revint.
　　Telle aventure li avint.
La nouvielle s'en espandi
Et li evesques l'entendy; 108
Si vot a tous priestres deffendre
Des saiaus a leur braies pendre.
Pour çou vous di au daarrains:
Priestres sont trop rade de rains, 112
Si en ont maint homme ahonté.
Maint conte vous en ai conté
Et par verités enquis ai;
Atant m'en tais, que plus n'en sai. 116

　　Explicit .c. et xvi. viers

NOTES

22. *meute* 'departure.' 'He was on the lookout for the butcher to set out.'

34. Ms *il y entroit troi s. h.* Tobler ended the discourse with vs 33 and corrected as follows: *il y entroient songneus homme*, an unacceptable emendation rejected by Scheler in favor of a more judicious solution: *Il a en toi trop songneus homme.*

42. The text printed by Tobler and followed by Scheler and by *MR* reads as follows:

> Coi se tenist viers le paroit.
> Et li bouciers se rendormi.
> . . . .
> Celle fu dou mains bien partie.

Scheler explained in a note: "La rime nous indique ici une lacune; cette lacune est-elle d'un seul vers ou des trois vers qui manquent à notre pièce d'après l'explicit du Ms. (*Explicit.c. et.xvi. viers*)? Cela est difficile à établir" (p. 122). But the manuscript does indeed read as printed here, and it was Tobler, not the scribe, who was responsible for the omission from vss 43 to 47. The explicit is then absolutely correct in regard to the number of verses contained in the work.

77. *Le denier Dieu* 'earnest money, deposit,' defined by Phillippe de Beaumanoir as follows: "noz entendons que marciés est fez si tost comme il est creantés a tenir...ou si tost que denier Dieu en est donés" (*T.-L.*, II, 1394). Cf. the *Pathelin* (Bowen, *Four Farces*, p. 64):

> Dieu sera
> Payé des premiers, c'est raison.
> 232 Vecy ung denier. Ne faison
> Rien qui soit ou Dieu ne se nomme.

It is possible though, in view of the fact that the butcher had not yet gone to his purse, that no money changed hands and that *doner le denier Dieu* was an expression that merely signaled the sealing of a bargain. Scheler (p. 410) speculates that he would have had small change elsewhere on his person.

78. *MR* read *bourse abrayer* and gloss the verb "ouvrir" (VI, 279). Neither Godefroy, *T.-L.*, nor the *FEW* records an example of *abrayer*, although the Bonnard-Salmon epitome of Godefroy (Paris-Leipzig, 1901) does list *abraier* "ouvrir," presumably following *MR*. This is surely a ghost word created by the editors of the *Recueil général* to be rejected in favor of Scheler's earlier reading *bourse a brayer* (but the scribe clearly wrote *braijer*) "bourse renfermée dans la ceinture des culottes" (p. 410).

102. *MR*'s misreading *entre .x. beus une brebis* completely destroys the image.

103. *Vois dou huihot*! 'Look at the cuckold!' A word of Picardo-Walloon provenance, *huihot* is unambiguously defined in a document dated 1397 quoted by Godefroy (*s.v. wihot*): "Tu n'oserois dire a ce compaignon la *huyho*, qui est a dire en françois coux." Jean also employed the word in another fabliau, *Du clerc qui fu repus deriere l'escrin* (*MR*, IV, pp. 51 and 52) as did the author of the *Farce de Frere Guillebert* (vs 445, see note).

111. Tobler erroneously read *vois di* and corrected to *vous di*, a correction repeated by Scheler and *MR*. The manuscript clearly reads *vous*.

2. Geoffroy de la Tour Landry

The *Livre du chevalier de la Tour Landry* (1371-1372)[1] is a collection of anecdotes and moral and religious precepts written by Geoffroy for the purpose of instructing his daughters. In Chapter LXII (pp. 127-28) he recounts a number of licentious tales about the wife of a rope-merchant, among which the following:

D'un bon homme qui estoit cordier

Aprés une aultre foiz lui avint que il cuida prendre une poche aux piez de son lit pour aler au marchié a trois leues d'illec, et il prist les brayes du prieur et les troussa a son eisselle. Et quant il fu au marchié et il cuida prendre sa poche, il prist les brayes dont il fut trop dolent et courouciè. Le prieur qui estoit cachié en la ruelle du lit, quant il cuida trouver ses brayes, il n'en trouva nulles fors la poche qui estoit de costé. Et lors il sceut bien que le mary les avoit prinses et emportees. Si fut la femme a grant meschief et ala a sa commere derechief et luy compta son fait et, por Dieu, que elle y meist remede; si lui dist:

—Vous prendrés unes brayes et je en prendray unes autres, et je lui diray que nous avons toutes brayes.

Et ainsi le firent. Et quand le preudomme fut revenu moult dolent et moult courouciez, sy vint la faulse commere le veoir et lui demanda quelle chiere il faisoit,

—car, mon compere, dist elle, je me doubte que vous n'ayez trouvé aucun mauvais encontre ou que vous n'aiez perdu du vostre.

—Vrayment, dist le bonhomme, je n'ay riens perdu, mais je ay bien autre pensee.

Et au fort elle fist tant qu'il luy dist comment il avoit trouvé unes brayes. Et quant elle l'ouy, elle commença a rire et a lui dire:

---

[1] Anatole de Montaiglon, *Le livre du chevalier de la Tour Landry pour l'enseignement de ses filles* (Paris, 1854).

—Ha! mon chier compere, or voy je bien que vous estes deceu et en voye d'estre tempté, car, par ma foy, il n'y a femme plus preudefemme en ceste ville que est la vostre ne qui se garde plus nettement envers vous que elle fait. Vrayment, elle et moy et aultres de ceste ville avons prises brayes pour nous garder de ces faulx ribaulx qui parfoiz prennent ces bonnes dames a cop; et, afin que vous sachiez que c'est verité, regardez se je les ay.

Et lors elle haulsa sa robe et luy monstra comment elle avoit brayes. Et il regarda et vit qu'elle avoit brayes et qu'elle disoit voir, si la crut. Et ainsi la faulce commere la sauva par deux foiz.

3. *La Farce de Frere Guillebert*

Described variously as "l'une des plus scandaleuses de celles qui nous sont restées,"[1] or "très licencieuse,"[2] the *Farce de Frere Guillebert* is nonetheless a most successful dramatic work from many points of view.[3] Its author demonstrates consummate technical skill in organizing the thematic elements and in the varied metrical devices employed in its composition. His use of the language is very effective in the raciness of the popular idiom and, in the manner of the *Pathelin*, the liberal mixture of dialect.

The *Guillebert* is preserved in a single gothic imprint of the sixteenth century, the famous *Recueil de Londres*, British Library, C.20.e.13. (*olim* C. 20. d).[4] The volume comprises a collection of forty-two farces plus six *sotties*, nine morality plays, three short mysteries, two *sermons joyeux*, a dramatic monologue and a debate, all printed separately and issuing from various presses around the middle of the sixteenth century. The format for all is the so-called *agenda*, oblong sheets (80 mm. x 286 mm.) printed for the use of actors or stage directors.[5] The *Guillebert* is the eighteenth piece in the collection and is made up of three folios (53d—55c), eight columns of text. There is no indication of place, date, or printer, and of course no

---

[1] Emmanuel Philipot, "Notice sur la *Farce de Frère Guillebert*," in *Mélanges de linguistique et de littérature romanes offerts à Mario Roques* (Paris, 1953), p. 237.

[2] L. Petit de Julleville, *Répertoire du théâtre comique en France au moyen âge* (Paris, 1886), p. 140. See also Barbara C. Bowen, "Metaphorical Obscenity in French Farce," *Comparative Drama* 2 (1977), 331-44, esp. p. 336.

[3] On the Middle French farce as a whole, see Barbara C. Bowen, *Les caractéristiques essentielles de la farce française et leur survivance dans les années 1550-1620* (Urbana, 1964).

[4] Published in facsimile with an introduction by Halina Lewicka, *Le Recueil du British Museum* (Genève, 1970).

[5] For a typographical description of this bound collection, see E. Droz, *Le Recueil Trepperel: Les sotties* (Paris, 1935), pp. 6-8.

mention of authorship. However, one other farce in the collection (no. 15), printed with the same fonts as the *Guillebert*, bears the following imprint: *Rouen, par Jehan de Prest demourant audict lieu*. This printer is known to have practiced his trade in Rouen from 1542 to 1559, and a Norman provenance for the play would agree with evidence from a study of the language and the colophon.

The period of activity of Jean de Prest would seem to preclude a date earlier than the middle of the century for the printing of the *Guillebert*. Nonetheless, certain critics have seen in the initials of the colophon, M. P. U. (which Montaiglon printed as M. P. V.), an indication of the date 1505. Emmanuel Philipot refutes this claim ("un P n'est pas un D; l'U a toute la rotondité qu'il fallait"),[6] and argues that the language of the farce is certainly later and that it betrays in all probability an influence from the works of Rabelais.[7] Also according to Philipot, certain features of the language demonstrate that the author sprinkled his text liberally with words from the Norman and Picard dialects. The colophon corroborates a Norman origin for the author: *Du jeune clergiè de Meulleurs*. Following Philipot this is obviously the parish of Meullers near Dieppe in the extreme northeast corner of the region of Bray; the town church is dedicated to Saint Valery whom Guillebert invokes in his misfortune. Furthermore, if the authorship of the farce is attributed to a young secular cleric of the church of Meullers, it would seem logical to assign the lecherous priest to the Mendicant order whose members "raflai[en]t à leurs concurrents des aumônes, des offrandes, des confessions" (pp. 238-39).

The verse structure of the *Guillebert* reveals an author of considerable skill and craftsmanship. For the most part it is written in octosyllabic rhymed couplets with, at the beginning, a variation to the pattern *abbcbc-*

---

[6]*Art. cit.,* p. 241.

[7]"Sans doute les preuves philologiques solides ne sont pas nombreuses et nous ne pouvons guère citer que *calibistris*, mot obscène qui ne se trouve pas dans la littérature avant Rabelais et *Guillebert*, et la locution *clystère barbarin* (v. 153) employée au sens érotique, dont les premiers exemples connus sont également de Rabelais et de *Guillebert*. Ajoutons que *fascher* (v. 340) dont le premier exemple connu (Bloch-W) est de 1511, ne se développe que lentement au XVIe siècle" (p. 241). He adds the adjective *encresté* (272) with the same obscene meaning as *acresté* in Rabelais (II, 1).

cdcdded etc. to vs 149 (with an occasional irregularity). The rhymes with few exceptions (but see 301, 379, 428-34, 437-39) are very regular if we take into consideration certain characteristics of sixteenth-century pronunciation (*e.g. aumoyres*: *meres* 20 or the Latin *vatum*: *baston* 346). While there are apparently numerous hyper- and hypometric verses if measured according to the rules of "correct" scansion, we must recall that the play was composed to be performed, not read, and the lines as spoken doubtless conformed to the octosyllable, except where a printer's error entailed a corrupt reading (*e.g.*, *devestes* 212 should probably be the imperative *deveste*, and vss 390, 466, 225, 450 are poorly transmitted). In some cases a slight correction, always inserted between brackets, reestablishes the syllable count. In the case of hypermetric verses, mute *e* often does not count (62, 63, 79, 378, 408, etc.), especially before a pause (127, 154, 183, 189, 208, 243, etc.). Atonic *je* (191, 257) and *que* (202, 494) elide; postposed *ce* and *de* lose their syllabic value: *peult ce* (224), *Que ce* (420), *fust ce* (443), *Est ce* (452), *Las! ce* (463), *et de* (292), etc.; interrogative *ou* is reduced to a *w*: *ou est* (284, 379, 381) is monosyllabic: *Il y a* (338, 467) is reduced to two syllables, and *il en* (496) to one, while conversely *a il* (371, 373) becomes the diphthong *ay*. Also reduced to two syllables are *j'ay esté* (305), *trouverra* (388) and *pendu a* (358), while the disyllabic form of the future is probably represented by *tuera* (386, cf. *turoit* 236). Hypometric verses can usually be rectified by supposing hiatus: *e.g.*, *-ion* (5, 6), *-ieulx* (9), etc., *ventrë* (56), *jasë* (107), etc. Within a verse *Guillebert* counts as either two (125, 308, 331, 409, 505) or three syllables (68, 297, 485).

The language of the *Frere Guillebert* is decidedly obscene, but the metaphoric pattern of this obscenity is imaginative and, like the *Pathelin*, appropriate to the theme and characters of the play. A fascination with sexual and scatological metaphor is manifest throughout the text.[8] Sexual intercourse is figuratively described as *faire zic zac* (13), *fouller* (13) and the pseudo-Latin *foullando* (1), *larder le connin* (28), *faire cela* (33), *fourbir le haubert* (70), *estrener le harnois* (72), *poindre* (86), *appoindre un coup* (91), *endurer des coups de la lance* (128), *faire le jeu* (133), *baulmer sur le tetin* (136), *herchier le patis* (140), *faire des coups* (162), *fourbir le custodinos* (311), *faire le bagaige* (319), *ferir* (328), *cauquer* (435), *fourbir le buihot* (444), and *rendre le debvoir* (478). The act itself is *hutin* (134), *causqueson* (167), and *hochement* (239); the male member a *Bidauldus* (3), *queue* (29), *instrument* (238), *outil* (270), *coquille* 281).

---

[8] Bowen, "Metaphorical Obscenity," p. 332.

appareil (325), *baston* (347), and of course the literal *vit* (389); and the testicles *couiller* (301), *tesniers* (356), and *coilles* (referring to the breeches as a *sac a coilles* 379). The vagina is a *calibistris* (1), *bouchan ventris* (2), *ventre* (9), *le bas* (17), *aumoyre* (20), *atellier* (27), *custodinos* (311), *orifice de la pance* (326), and *buihot* (444). But Bowen, "Metaphorical Obscenity," pp. 332-33, argues that these expressions and metaphors, far from being brutal or grotesque, are essentially human in their playfulness—natural, comic, and even poetic. She finds them especially comical by their very profusion and because of the fact that most, such as 'polishing a hauberk,' or 'strike with a lance,' are socially inappropriate for the Friar.

Characteristic of many farces is the introductory monologue, but in the case of the *Guillebert* it is unusual in that it takes the form of a *sermon joyeux* (Bowen, *Caractéristiques*, pp. 59-60). In the best tradition of pulpit oratory it opens with a text which provides the theme to be developed in the course of the sermon.[9] The text here is, predictably, an obscene parody resembling a scriptural passage.[10]

On three occassions the author skillfully incorporates lyric poems of a fixed form into the text, all spoken by Friar Guillebert. The first of two ballades terminates the *sermon joyeux* (25-73) and is thematically connected to the text of the sermon; the second, a mock will in the manner of Villon's *Testament*, is spoken by the frightened Minorite who fears the punishment inflicted on Abelard and who laments his former sexual transgressions (302-336). Finally, a rondeau, presumably sung by Guillebert at the joyous prospect of attaining his goal, is inserted just before the husband sets out for the market (192-205).

Other stylistic devices employed by the author include the use of stichomythian verses (177, 192, 292, etc.) and rondeau-like refrains which are characteristic of the genre as a whole (Bowen, *Caractéristiques*,

---

[9] See, for example, Robert of Basevorn's *Forma praedicandi* in James J. Murphy, *Three Medieval Rhetorical Arts* (Berkeley, 1971), pp. 109-215, where the treatise on the thematic sermon takes the form of such a sermon, opening with a text to be amplified.

[10] A study of this literary sub-form is now available in Sandra L. Gilman, *The Parodic Sermon in European Perspective* (Wiesbaden, 1974), esp. pp. 1-30.

pp. 71-72): *Dieu vous gard, ma commere Agnès* (74, 77, 80), or *Et dont vient mon jeune tetot* (142, 145, 148). The interspersion of Latin, sometimes latinate French, is particularly appropriate both to the character of the cleric on stage and to the clerical audience. Like the author of *Les Braies au cordelier*, the author of the farce injects on one occasion a parodic dimension to the dialogue in the discrepancy it establishes between the courtly and refined language of the Friar in pleading his case and the inappropriateness of this language to the characters and situation (119-24).

The *Farce de Frere Guillebert* was published on one previous occasion by Anatole de Montaiglon in Vol. I of M. Viollet le Duc, *Ancien théâtre françois* (Paris, 1854), pp. 305-27 (Vols. I-III contain the entire *Recueil de Londres*). Montaiglon's edition, as indeed all of those he edited for the *Ancien théâtre françois*, has been severely criticized for its many misreadings of the original; the editor failed to understand many passages and he provided no commentary whatsoever to the text. The present edition is based on the facsimile of the *Recueil de Londres* published by Halina Lewicka.

FARCE NOUVELLE DE FRERE GUILLEBERT

Tresbonne et fort joyeuse a quatre personages
c'est assavoir

Frere Guillebert
l'Homme vieil
Sa Femme jeune
La Commere.

FRERE GUILLEBERT COMMENCE.

53d
Foullando in calibistris,
Intravit per bouchan ventris
Bidauldus, purgando renes.

    Noble assistence, retenez 4
Ces motz pleins de devotion;
C'est touchant l'incarnation
De l'ymage de la brayette
Qui entre corps, aureille, et teste 8
Au precïeulx ventre des dames.
Si demandez entre voz, femmes:
"Or ça, beau pere, *quomodo*?
Le texte dict que *foullando,* 12
En foullant et faisant zic zac,
Le gallant se trouve au bissac.
Entendez vous bien, mes fillettes?
S'on s'encroue sur voz mamelettes 16
Et qu'on vous chatouille le bas,
N'en sonnez mot, ce sont esbatz,
Et n'en dictes rien a voz meres.
De quoy serviroient voz aumoyres 20
Si ne vouliez bouter dedenz?
Se vous couchez tousjours a dens,
Jamais n'aurez les culz meurtris
Foullando in calibistris. 24

    Gentilz gallans de rond bonnet
Aymantz le [se]xe feminin,
Gardez se l'atellier est net

Devant que larder le connin, 28
Car s'on prent en queue le venin,
On est pirs qu'au trou sainct Patris
Foullando in calibistris.

Tetins moussus, doulces fillettes 32
Qui aimez bien faire cela,
Et en branlant voz mamelettes
Jamais [vous] ne direz holla;
Un point y est, guettez vous la, 36
Que vous n'ayez *fructus ventris*
Foullando in calibistris.

Vous, jeunes dames marïees
Qui n'en avez pas a demy, 40
. . . .
N'escondissez point un amy,
Car c'est, et fust il endormy,
Au papar ceulx qui son[t] pestris 44
Foullando in calibistris.

Je vous recommande a mon prosne,
Tous noz freres de robe grise.
Je vous promectz, c'est belle aumosne 48
Que faire bien a gens d'eglise;
Grans pardons a, je vous advise,
A leur prester *bouchan ventris*
Foullando in calibistris. 52

Plusïeurs beaulx testins espiés
Se font batre sans nul mercy,
Et puis qu'ilz ont des petis piedz
Au ventrë, ilz sont en soucy. 56
Las! [s]e disent, d'ou vient cecy?
Et le veulx tu sçavoir, Bietris?
Intravit per bouchan ventris.

Un tas de vieilles esponnees 60
Qui vous font tant de preudefemmes,
Il semble qu'ilz soient estonnees
S'ilz oyent parler qu'on ayme dames;

Et vous croyez que les infames 64
Ont tous les bas espoitronnez
De servir *purgando renes.*

   Mes dames, je vous recommande
Le povre frere Guillebert; 68
Se l'une de vous me demande
Pour fourbir un poy son haubert,
Approchez, car g'y suis expert;
Plusieurs harnois ay estrenez, 72
Bidauldus, purgando renes.

    LA FEMME *Commence*

54*a*   Dieu vous gard, ma commere Agnés,
Et vous doing santé et soulas.
        LA COMMERE
Ha! ma commere, bien venez. 76
        LA FEMME
Dieu vous gard, ma commere Agnés.
        LA COMMERE
Que maigre et palle devenez;
Qu'avez vous, ma commere, helas!
        LA FEMME
Dieu vous gard, ma commere Agnés, 80
Et vous doint santé et soulas,
Que cent foys morte me souhaitte.
        LA COMMERE
Et pourquoy?
        LA FEMME
        D'estre mise es lacz
D'un vieillart et ainsi subjette. 84
De jour, de nuict je vous souhette,
Mais de poindre c'est peu ou point.
Quel plaisir a une fillette
A qui le gentil tetin point? 88
        LA COMMERE
Sçait il plus rien du bas pourpoint?
        LA FEMME
Helas! m'amye, il s'est cassé.
S'en un moys un coup est appoint,
Il [en] est ainsi tost lassé. 92

Je l'ay beau tenir embrassé...
Tout autant de goust qu'en vieil lard.
Mauldict soit il qui a brassé
Me marïer a tel vieillard! 96
Quel plaisir d'ung tel papelard
Pour avoir en amour pasture.
LA COMMERE
Il vous fault un amy gaillard
Pour supplïer a l'escripture. 100
Dieu n'entend point, aussi Nature,
Que jeunes dames ayent souffrette,
Mais cherchez une creature
Qui ayt la langue un poy segrette. 104
LA FEMME
Il est [bien] vray; quant on en quette,
On est regardé de travers;
Mais quoy qu'on jasë ou barbette,
Je jouray de bref a l'anvers. 108
Doibt mon beau cors pourrir en vers
Sans voir ce que faisoit ma mere?
Vienne, fust il moyne ou convers,
Je luy presteray mon aumoyre.
LA COMMERE
Enda! c'est bien dict, ma commere,
J'en ay faict a mon temps ainsi;
C'est une chose bien amere
De languir tousjours en soucy. 116
LA FEMME
Adieu donc, je m'en voys d'icy
En attendant quelque advantage.

FRERE GUILLEBERT
Ma dame, ayez de moy mercy
Ou mourir me fault avant aage; 120
Mon las coeur vous baille en ostage,
Plaise vous le mettre a son aise.
Je vous dis en poy de langaige
Ce qui me tient en grant mesaise. 124
LA FEMME
Frere Guillebert, ne vous desplaise,
Ce n'est pas ainsi qu'on amanche.

FRERE GUILLEBERT
M'amye, je vous pry qu'il vous plaise
Endurer trois coups de la lance; 128
C'est belle osmosne sans doubtance
Donner pour Dieu aux souffretteux.
  LA FEMME
S'on savoit nostre accointance,
Mes gens me saqueroient les yeulx. 132
  FRERE GUILLEBERT
He! nous ferons si bien noz jeux
Qu'on ne sçaura rien du hutin.
S'une foys je suys sur mes oeufz,
Je baulmeray sur le tetin. 136
  LA FEMME
Venez donc demain bien matin;
J'envoyray Marin au marché.
  FRERE GUILLEBERT
Plaisir sera au vieil mastin
De trouver son patis herchié. 140
  LA FEMME
Le vieillart a trop bon marché.

  L'HOMME
Et dont vient mon jeune tetot?
Je vous ay toute jour cherché.
  LA FEMME
Que me voulez [vous donc] si tost? 144
  L'HOMME
Et d'ou vient mon jeune teto[t]?
Que vous engamez ung petiot.
  LA FEMME
Vostre bas est trop eslanché.
  L'HOMME
Et d'ou vient mon jeune tetot? 148
Je vous ay toute jour cherché.
  LA FEMME
Enda! j'ay le coeur si faché
Que vouldrois estre en purgatoire.
  L'HOMME
Vous fault il ung suppositoire 152
Ou [ung] clistere barbarin?

LA FEMME
Vous m'avez abusee, Marin;
Avec vous je vis en langueur.
L'HOMME
Je ne vous bas ne fais rigueur; 156
Demandez moy s'il vous fault rien.
LA FEMME
Ce n'est point, vous n'entendez rien
La ou me tient la maladie;
Voulez vous que je le vous die? 160
Je suis par trop jeune pour vous.
L'HOMME
En ung moys je fais mes cinq coups,
La sepmaine ung coup justement.
LA FEMME
Cela n'est qu[e] afemmement; 164
J'aymerois tout aussi cher rien.
L'HOMME
Comment? vous vous passïez bien
De causqueson chez vostre mere.
LA FEMME
La douleur est bien plus amere; 168
Mourir de soif emprés le puis.
L'HOMME
Je fais tout le mieulx que je puis;
J'en suis, par Dieu, tout strebatu.
Combien que j'aye combatu, 172
Encor vous dictes estre enceinte.
LA FEMME
Ç'a esté de prïe[r] une saincte,
Que pleine suis de peu de chose.
Encor[e] dire ne vous ose; 176
Sçais bien quoy?
L'HOMME
Et dictes, becire.
LA FEMME
Marin, mon amy, je desire...
Las! je crains tant le povre fruict.
L'HOMME
Dictes le moy, soit cru ou cuit 180
Vous me verrez courir la rue.

LA FEMME
Je desire de la morue
Fresche, des moules, du pain mollet,
Et si vouldrois bien d'ung collet   184
D'ung gras montom et d'ung vin doulx;
Et si, Marin, entendez vous
De cela qui estoit si blanc
Quant nous marïames?
L'HOMME
             Du flan?   188
LA FEMME
Et voyre, vous y estes tout droict;
Je n'en puis durer [or]endroit.
L'HOMME
Je iray donc demain bien matin
Au marché.

FRERE GUILLEBART
Rondeau
        He! gentil tetin,   192
Que tant tu me tiens en l'oreille.
Pour une qui s'appareille,

Ung vray chef d'oeuvre de Nature,
Mon corps veulx mettre a l'aventure;   196
A les sangler pour la pareille
Mon corps et membres j'appareille,
N'escondire pas creature
Pour une [qui s'appareille].   200

54*c*   Si ton mari dort ou il veille,
Mais que accés j'aye a la figure,
Je veulx que l'on me defigure
Se point un grain je m'esmerveille,   204
Pour une [qui s'appareille].

L'HOMME
Il est [ja] temps que je m'esveille;
Adieu, je m'en vois au marché.
LA FEMME
Adieu, et prenez bon marché,   208

Mais je vous prie, n'oubliez rien.
   L'HOMME
Nennin non, il m'en souvient bien.

  FRERE GUILLEBART
Hola, hay! je viens bien a point.
   LA FEMME
Oy! devestes chausses et pourpoint   212
Et approchez, la place est chaulde.
  FRERE GUILLEBART *se despouille*
Au moins y a il point de fraulde?
Je crains la touche, sur mon ame.
   LA FEMME
Pas n'estes digne d'avoir dame   216
Puis que vous estes si paoureux.

   L'HOMME
Et suis je point bien malheureux
D'avoir oublïé mon bissac?
Je n'ay pennier, pouche, ne sac;   220
Il fault bien tost que je m'en aille
Requerir le mien, hay, hola!

  FRERE GUILLEBART
Et vertu sainct Gens, qu'esse la?
Monsieur sainct Françoys, que peult ce estre?   224
   LA FEMME
Par enda! c'est nostre maistre;
Je croy qu'il se doubte du jeu.
  FRERE GUILLEBART
Que c'est vostre homme, vertu bieu;
Helas! je suys bien malheureux.   228
Le Dyable m'a faict amoureux
Je croy, ce n'a pas esté Dieu.
   LA FEMME
Muchez vous tost en quelque lieu!
S'il vous trouve, vous estes frit.   232
  FRERE GUILLEBERT
Et, mon Dieu, je suis bien destruit;
Vertu sainct Gens, le cul me tremble.
Or ça, s'il nous trouvoit ensemble,

    Me turoit il a vostre advis?   236
            LA FEMME
Jamais pire homme je ne vis,
Et si crains bien vostre instrument.
        FRERE GUILLEBERT
Le Dyable ayt part au hochement
Et a toute la cauqueson.   240
Accoustré seray en oyson;
Je n'auray plus au cul que plume.
            LA FEMME
S'il est en gaignë, il escume;
Semble a, veoir, ung homme desvé.   244
        FRERE GUILLEBERT
He! *Pater Noster* et *Ave*!
Vertu bieu, je suis bien hoché.
            LA FEMME
Las! mon amy, c'est trop presché;
Venez ça, je vous mucheray.   248
        FRERE GUILLEBERT
Qui m'en croira, je m'en fuyray,
Par Dieu, le cas, bien entendu.
            LA FEMME
Mais que soyés bien estendu,
Point ne vous voirra soubz ce coffre.   252
        FRERE GUILLEBERT
Or ça, donc, puis que le cas s'offre,
Me voicy bouté a l'acul;
Et couvrez moy un poy le cul,
Je sens bien le vent qui me frappe.   256
S'une foys du danger je eschape,
S'on m'y ra, je seray asseur.
            LA FEMME
Taisez vous, n'ayez point de peur,
Je vous serviray, si je puis.   260

            L'HOMME
Et puys, hay! m'ouvrirez vous l'huis?
            LA FEMME
54*d*   Las! mon amy, qui vous ramaine?
        FRERE GUILLEBERT
Il me fault cy estendre en raine;

Qu'au Dyable soit il ramené. 264
    L'HOMME
Ne suis je point bien fortuné?
J'avois oublïé mon bissac.
   FRERE GUILLEBERT
A ce coup je suis a bazac;
Je suis, par Dieu, couché dessus. 268
Et sainct Fremin et puis Jesus,
C'est faict, helas! du povre outil.
Vray Dieu, il estoit si gentil
Et si gentement encresté. 272
    LA FEMME
Je vous l'avois hier apresté
Sur ce coffre avant que coucher.
    L'HOMME
Couchez vous, je le voys chercher,
Et gardez vous que n'ayez froid. 276
   FRERE GUILLEBERT
Il s'en vient, par Dieu, cy tout droict.
He! sainct Valery, qu'esse cy?
Ha! s'il me prenoit en mercy
Et qu'il print toute ma robille... 280
Mais, helas! perdre la coquille!
Mon Dieu, c'est pour fienter par tout.
    LA FEMME
Ne cerchez point la, vers ce bout,
Il n'y est point.
    L'HOMME
      Et ou est il don? 284
   FRERE GUILLEBERT
Mon Dieu, je demande pardon,
Tout fin plat je te cry mercy.
    L'HOMME
On sent, par Dieu, cy le vessy;
Vertu sainct Gens, quel puanteur! 288
   FRERE GUILLEBERT
Et on faict sa malle puteur;
S'il estoit aussi tourmenté,
Il eust, par Dieu, pieça fienté.
    LA FEMME
Et puis l'av'ous, Marin?

L'HOMME
                Ouy, et de beaulx;   292
Point n'est cy parmy ses drapeaulx.
On l'a quelque part mis en mue.
       FRERE GUILLEBERT
Je suys mort si je me remue.
J'ay desja le cul descouvert.   296
Et pour ce, frere Guillebert,
Mourras tu si piteusement?
Deux motz feray de testament
Devant que laisser m'accueillir   300
Et quant m'ait couppé le couiller:

   A Cupido, dieu d'amourettes,
Je laisse mon ame a pourveoir
Pour la mettre avec des fillettes,   304
Car j'ay esté bien aise a les veoir.
La dame aura mon coeur, pour veoir,
Pour qui me fault icy perir.
Frere Guillebert, te fault il mourir?   308

   Tetins poinctifz comme linotz
Qui portent faces angelicques,
Pour fourbir leur custodinos
Auront l'ymage et mes brelicques;   312
Ne les logez point parmy flicques,
Dedens jambons les fault nourrir.
Frere Guillebert, te fault il mourir?

   Jeunes dames, friantz tetotz,   316
Vous aurez mes brayes pour tout gaige
Pour vous fourbir un poy le dos
Quant vous avez faict le bagaige;
Frotez rains et ventre, g'y gaige,   320
Cela vous fera recourir.
Frere Guillebert, te fault il mourir?

   Aux muguetz, grateurs de pareilz,
Laisse ma derniere ordonnance,   324
Qu'on leur fera leurs appareilz
Sur l'orifice de la pance
De leurs femmes, s'en est la chance;

Ilz en auront plus beau ferir. 328
Frere Guillebert, te fault il mourir?

Je prie a tous ses bons yvrongnes,
Se frere Guillebert est trespassé,
Qu'ilz disent en lavant leurs brongnes, 332
J'ay bien gardé le temps passé,
. . . .
Mon gentil gosier de sorir.
Frere Guillebert, te fault il mourir? 336

L'HOMME
Je ne sçay plus ou le querir;
Il y a de la dyablerie.
LA FEMME
Parlez de la vierge Marie;
L'HOMME
Vertu bieu, je suis trop fasché, 340
Si fault il qu'il soit cy caché.
FRERE GUILLEBERT
In manus tuas, Domine,
Nisi quia, Domine, ne
Tedet spiritus et pelli, 344
Confiteor Deo celi
Ut queant quod chorus vatum...
He! te perdray je, beau baston?
C'est faict ce coup, povre couiller; 348
Il vient, par Dieu, tout droict fouiller
Cy sur moy; et, vertu sainct Gens,
Fault il tuer ainsi les gens?
Par Dieu, je varie de crïer; 352
Gaignerois je rien a prïer
Et a luy monstrer ma couronne?
He! mon Dieu, comme tu me gravonnes!
Adieu gentilz tesniers pelus. 356
LA FEMME
Mon amy, ne cherchez la plus;
Qu'est cela pendu a cest cheville?
L'HOMME
Et ça, au Dyable, ça c'est ille.
Venez, que vous vous faictes chercher. 360

Nota qu'il doit prendre le hault de chaulses a
Frere Guillebert pour son bissac

      FRERE GUILLEBERT
Encor pourray je bien hocher.
Vertu sainct Gens, que je suis aise.
      L'HOMME
Adieu m'amye, que je vous baise
Ung poy a mon departement.   364
      LA FEMME
N'espargnez point l'esbatement.
      L'HOMME
Je feray le cas au retour.
      FRERE GUILLEBERT
Par sainct Gens, revoycy bon tour;
Encor pourra paistre pelee.   368
      LA FEMME
Helas! j'estois bien desolee,
Je cuydois qu'il vous mist a sac.
      FRERE GUILLEBERT
Ou gibet a il prins ce bissac?
J'estoit, par Dieu, couché dessus.   372
      LA FEMME
Et qu'a il donc apporté, Jesus?
Il sera bien tost cy rapoint.
      FRERE GUILLEBERT
Par Dieu, si ne m'y rair'ous point;
Ronge cul ravoir sainct Françoys.   376
Par nostre Dame, je m'en vois
Mais que j'aye reprins ma despoille.
Vertu Dieu, ou est mon sac a coilles?
Comment? je ne le trouve point.   380
      LA FEMME
Ou est[oit] il?
      FRERE GUILLEBERT
            Emprés mon pourpoint
Pendu cy en ceste cheville.
      LA FEMME
He! vierge Marie, ce sont ille
Qu'il a prins en lieu de bissac.   384
Las! mon Dieu, je suis a bazac;

Il me tuera mais qu'il le voye.
FRERE GUILLEBERT
Ma foy, je m'en voys mettre en voye,
Je croy qu'il ne m'y trouverra point.   388
Je prandray mon vit a mon poing,
Mes mains me serviront de brayette.
LA FEMME
Helas! et suis je bien meffaicte?
N'est ce point bien icy malheur?   392
En amours je n'euz jamais eur;
Las! je ne sçay que deviendray.
M'enfuyray je ou l'atendray?
Se je l'atens, il me tuera.   396
Je m'en vois veoir que me dira
Ma commere. Helas! Dieu vous gard.

LA COMMERE
Que vous avez piteux regard;
Vous n'avez pas esté bastue?   400
LA FEMME
Helas! m'amye, je suis perdue,
Je ne sçauray que devenir.
LA COMMERE
Bo! il ne fault point tant gemir;
A tous maulx on trouve remede.   404
LA FEMME
Donnez moy [tost] conseil et ayde,
Aultrement je suis mise a sac.
Las! m'amye, en lieu de bissac
Nostre homme a prins comme bien expert   408
Les brayes de frere Guillebert,
plorando
Et s'en va atout au marché.
LA COMMERE
Cela, mon Dieu, c'est bien chïé;
N'est ce aultre chose qui vous point?   412
LA FEMME
Ha! vous ne le congnoissez point;
Il dira que j'en fais beaucoup,
Et si jamais qu'un povre coup
N'en fist par le prix de mon ame.   416

LA COMMERE
N'est ce aultre chose, nostre Dame?
Allez vous en a la maison,
Je luy prouveray par raison
Que ce sont les brayes sainct Françoys. 420
Tenez gestes, je m'y en vois;
Qu'on me fesse se ne l'appaise.
[LA FEMME]
He! mon Dieu, que me faictes aise;
Je m'en voys trotant bien menu. 424

L'HOMME
Me voicy donc tantost venu,
Mais je suis quasi estouffé
Tant se bissac sent l'eschauffé.
Et, vertu sainct Gens, qu'esse cy? 428
Bissac? Bissac, par Dieu, non est,
C'est l'abit d'un cul gueres net,
Car y voycy l'estuy a couilles.
En voulez vous menger des moules? 432
Me le faict on belle fresaye?
Se je vous tiens, je vous asseure,
Le Dyable vous cauquera bien.
Le Diable enport se j'en fais rien, 436
Que n'ayez le gosier couppé.
Hon, me voicy bien atourné.
Le margout, quand suis retourné,
Estoit muché en quelque lieu. 440
Ne te sçavois je, vertu Dieu,
Je vous eusse bien foutiné,
Par Dieu, et fust ce ung *domine*.
Vous faictes fourbir le buihot 444
Et on m'appellera huihot.
Et, par Dieu, j'en seray vengé.
Le grant Diable m'a bien engé
De vostre corps, belle bourgeoise. 448
LA COMMERE
Mon compere, vous faictes grand noyse;
On ne vous a faict rien?
L'HOMME
Vertu bieu, on m'en baille bien.

Est ce ainsi qu'on envoye les gens; 452
Hon, hon, cauquer, vertu sainct Gens,
La cauqueson sera amere.
    LA COMMERE
Et pensez vous que ma commere
Voulsist, helas! se mesporter? 456
    L'HOMME
Le Diable le puist emporter!
Voyez, voyla sa preudhomie.
    monstrat caligas
    LA COMMERE
Las! mon amy, ne pensez mye
Qu'il y ait icy de la fault. 460
Le coeur dedens mon ventre saute
Quand manïer je vous les vois.
Las! ce sont les brayes sainct Françoys,
Ung si precïeux reliquere. 464
    L'HOMME
Et, vertu sainct Gens, a quoy faire
Les eust on mises a ma maison?
    LA COMMERE
Vrayement, il y a bien raison,
Et pensez vous bien, Dieux avant, 468
Que vous eussiez faict un enfant
Sans l'aide du sainct reliquaire?
    L'HOMME
Et pourquoy n'en sçaurois je faire?
    LA FEMME
Helas! vous estes esprouvé. 472
    L'HOMME
Encor, par Dieu, suis estonné
Comme cecy y peult servir.
    LA COMMERE
Quant du joyau en peult chevir,
Il en fault froter rains et pance 476
Sept foys et dire sa creance,
Puis aprez rendre le debvoir.
On ne les cuidasmes onc avoir;
Encor, s'on ne nous eust congneues, 480
Jamais nous ne les eussions eues;
Et si, da, les fault renvoyer.

L'HOMME
Je les yray donc convoyer
Moy mesmes jusques au couvent. 484
LA COMMERE
Frere Guillebert vient souvent,
Il ne les luy fault que bailler.
L'HOMME
Or bien donc, il s'en fault aller
Pour veoir qu'en dira nostre femme. 488
Pardonnez moy, par nostre Dame,
M'amye, j'ay failly lourdement.

LA COMMERE
Vous ne sçavez pas, voyrement,
Qu'il estimoit de vous, m'amye? 492
Le bon homme ne pensoit mye
Que eussiez les brayes sainct Françoys,
Et en faisoit tout plain d'effrois;
Il ne sçavoit comme il en estoit. 496
LA FEMME
Le coeur bien me l'admonnestoit
Quand les ay trouvees ceans.
J'aymerois mieulx pourrir en fiens
Que ne me daigner mesporter. 500
LA COMMERE
M'amye, il les fault reporter.
LA FEMME
Las! voyre, il nous ont bien servis.

L'HOMME
Par Dieu, m'amye, ja n'y pensis
Qu'a ceste heure cy, Dieu avant... 504
LA COMMERE
C'est frere Guillebert la devant;
Il vault mieulx les luy bailler.
L'HOMME
C'est bien dict. Venez cy parler
Un petit, s'il vous plaist, beau pere. 508
FRERE GUILLEBERT
A t'on ceans de moy affaire?
Je croy que ouy, comme je voys.
LA FEMME
Ce sont les choses sainct Françoys

Que remporterez, s'il vous plaist. 512
        FRERE GUILLEBERT
Je le feray sans plus de plaict,
Mais boutez vous tous a genoulx
Affin que le sainct prie pour nous;
Et si vous fault baiser tous trois 516
Les brayes de monsieur sainct Françoys,
Vous aurez l'alaine plus doulce.
        LA FEMME
Baillez m'en une bonne touche
Puis qu'en ay eu si grand doulceur. 520
        FRERE GUILLEBERT
C'est tresbien faict, ma bonne seur,
Car c'est un fort beau reliquere.
        L'HOMME
Allons les reporter, beau pere,
Que chascun voyse a son degré. 524
        FRERE GUILLEBERT
Adieu, messieurs, prenez en gre.

        FINIS
Du jeune clergié de Meulleurs
        M P U.

NOTES

1. An obscene Franco-Latin text to the parodic sermon: *Foullando*, a Latinized gerund from *fouller* 'to trample, full,' with obscene meaning; *calibistris*, of unknown origin, 'vulva,' first found in Rabelais: *Les calibistrys des femmes de ce pays sont a meilleur marché que les pierres* (II, 15); *Intravit per bouchan ventris* 'entered the opening of the belly' (with surely a pun on *entra vit*); *Bidauldus*, from *bidet* 'little nag' or 'small pistol,' the male member (cf. Cotgrave: *Bidet de culbute. Membre viril*); *purgando renes* 'to purge the bladder.'

11. *quomodo* 'in what manner, how?'

14. *se trouver au bissac* 'be undone;' cf. *être à la besace* 'être ruiné' (*Dic. Gen.*).

16. *s'encrouer* 'catch, cling, fondle,' of Norman origin (Philipot, p. 239).

17. Cf. Huguet, s.v. *conin* 2: *Sotz qui chassent nuyt et jour aux congnins, Sotz qui ayment à frequenter le bas.*

20. *aumoyre* 'coffer, cupboard,' with obscene meaning.

21. *bouter* 'plunge.'

28. *larder le connin* 'dress the rabbit with bacon,' an obscene metaphor (from the pun *connin-con*) for sexual intercourse (probably an alteration of *larder l'oye*). Cf. Charles d'Orléans: *Quant aux connins que dittes qu'ay amez, Ilz sont pour moy, plusieurs ans a passez, Mis en oubly* (ed. Pierre Champion [Paris, 1956], p. 136).

29. Cf. the proverb cited by Nicot: *En la queuë gist le venin,* translated *Ultima mortiferum conservat cauda venerum.* Similar proverbs are found in M. Le Roux de Lincy, *Le livre des proverbes français* (Paris, 1859), II, 198.

30. *trou sainct Patris*, a reference to the Purgatory of Saint Patrick described by Marie de France in her *Espurgatoire saint Patriz* (ed. T.

A. Jenkins [Chicago, 1903], vss 305-08) as *Une fosse [qui] estoit obscure, Espoëntable a desmesure.*

32. *moussus* 'downy, silky.' See Cotgrave, *s.v. Mousse:* "The mossie downe that grows upon Quinces, Peaches."

33. Frequent euphemism in the farce; cf. Bowen (*le Cuvier*): *Et puis faire cela Aulcunesfois a l'eschappee* (vss 141-42).

36. *guettez vous la* 'be careful of this' (Philipot, p. 239).

37. *fructus ventris* 'fruit of the womb, pregnancy,' doubtless an echo of the *Ave Maria* based on Luke 1: 42: *Benedicta tu inter mulieres et benedictus fructus ventris tui.*

43. *C'est...Au papar ceulx qui sont pestris*; the meaning is unclear. Philipot, p. 240, glosses *papar* "papa, père putatif" and explains: "la distinction entre père et papa ressort nettement de deux vers de la farce picarde d'un Amoureus (A. Th. Fr. I, 222). Mais on trouve aussi *papar* et *papart* en picard et en rouchi...au sens d'enfant, poupart."

46. *prosne* (PROXIMUM) 'one close, neighbor.'

47. *freres de robe grise* 'Grey Friars, Franciscans.'

53. *espiés* "resembling an eare of corne" (Cotgrave); "ayant des épis formés" (Huguet).

55. "*ilz* apparait assez fréquemment au féminin pluriel;" Christiane Marchello-Nizia, *Histoire de la langue française au XIVe et XVe siècles* (Paris, 1979), p. 175.

60. *esponnees* 'worn out.' Huguet gives only this passage with a question mark, but see Philipot, p. 239: "fatigué, éreinté: du norman pone, ventre; poule esponnée = poule épuisée à force de pondre."

65. *espoitronnez* 'uncovered, bare;' cf. Cotgrave, *s.v. Espoitronnement:* "A discouering of the bosome, a going open breasted."

72. Huguet records for *estrenez* only the usual meaning "étrenner," but see Cotgrave, *s.v. Estrener:* "to beat, swindge, cudgell, correct."

85. Correct to *je le souhette*?

94. *lard* 'fat of bacon or pork.'

97. *papelard* "an hipocrite, a dissembler; a flatterer" (Cotgrave). See Ronald N. Walpole, "On the Etymology of Old French *papelard*," *Romance Philology* 22 (1969), 492-97.

98. *avoir pasture* 'put out to pasture, retire' where love is concerned?

100. *supplïer a l'escripture* 'add to, make up for.' Huguet, *s. v. supployer*, glosses "suppléer." For the erotic sense, cf. *Les Cents Nouvelles Nouvelles* (ed. F. Sweetser [Genève-Paris, 1966]): *je pourray bien pescher en vostre escriptoire* (XXIII, 58).

102. *souffrette* "Need, penurie, pouertie, scarcite, want of necessarie means" (Cotgrave).

107. *jasë*, cf. Cotgrave, *s. v. Iaser*: "To prate, prattle, babble;" *barbette* "mutter, murmure."

108. *jouray*, reduced future of *jouer* (Marchello-Nizia, p. 223).

126. *amanche* (= *emmanche*) 'set a handle on,' hence 'arrange, make right.' The verse means 'that is no way to go about it.' The rhyme *amanche: lance* (128) is Normano-Picard (Philipot, p. 239).

130. *souffretteux* 'those in need.' 'It is a fine thing to give alms for God's sake to the needy' (see n. 102).

132. *saqueroient* (OF *sachier*) 'tear out.'

134. *hutin* 'squabble, quarrel,' with obscene meaning.

135. *estre sur ses oeufz* 'get down to business,' an expression not found in Huguet. The image is that of a hen setting her eggs.

136. Philipot, p. 239, would correct to *haumeray* "frapper," derived from *heaume*.

139. *mastin* "a rude, filthie, currish or cruell fellow" (Cotgrave).

140. *herchië* 'harrowed;' *patis* 'pasture ground,' hence 'to find his field plowed, worked over.'

143. On *toute jour* see Foulet, *Glossaire*, p. 156: "Quoique *jor* soit masculin, il s'est constitué une locution calquée sur *tote nuit* où il est féminin."

146. *engamez*; Huguet cites only this passage with a question mark.

147. *eslanché* "limp, meager" (Philipot, p. 239). Cf. Huguet, *s. v. eslancé*: "La mandragore. . .rend les hommes lasches, tristes et *eslancés*, mornes et sans aucune force."

153. *clistere barbarin* 'rough or violent clyster, injection.' Cf. Rabelais: *Je luy appreste un clystère barbarin* (III, 34), translated by Cotgrave "I will provide for her bellie a plaister of warm guts," a colorful translation repeated by Urquhart and Le Motteux.

164. *afemmement* 'unmanly.' Huguet lists only the verb *afemmir* "s'efféminer."

167. *causqueson*; see Philipot, p. 239: "action de cauquer. Godefroy ne cite que nos trois exemples. . . . Serait-ce une création individuelle? En tous cas la forme normande correcte serait *cauquechon*." However, Cotgrave does list Norman *cauquer* and Picard *cauquier* with the meaning "to tread a henne, as a cocke doth" and cites the proverb: "Quand la fille pese un auque (= goose), on luy peut mettre la cauque." Huguet provides many examples of *caucher* "presser, fouler, couvrir la femelle." Sixteenth-century *cauquemare* often signified *incubus*.

169. For this well-known paradox, see Villon's so-called *Ballade du concours de Blois*: "Je meurs de suef auprés de la fontaine" (in P. Champion's edition of the poetry of Charles d'Orléans, p. 156). On the *concours*, see now R. E. V. Stuip, "Je meurs de soif et suy a la fontaine," in *Mélanges de linguistique et de littérature offerts à Lein Geschiere* (Amsterdam, 1975), pp. 25-36.

171. *strebatu*; Huguet lists only this example with a question mark. Perhaps it is a fanciful compound of *batu* with something like Latin *strenuus* 'vigorous.'

177. *becire*; see Philipot, p. 240: "beau sire. Formule curieuse, adressée par le mari à sa femme." But see a similar formula in Old Provençal *midons* (MEUS DOMINUS) addressed to a woman.

179. Imp. *crarins*.

184. *collet d'ung montom* 'neck of a sheep.' Philipot, p. 240, ascribes *monton* to the Norman dialect.

215. *il craint la touche* "His cause, or conscience, naught, makes him avoid all triall" (Cotgrave, *s.v. touche*). Huguet glosses *craindre la touche* "craindre les coups, avoir peur" and cites the proverb: "Il est de bas or, il craind la touche," a pun on *pierre de touche*.

231. *muchez* 'hide.'

232. *frit* 'fried,' hence 'done for.' Cf. *Les Cents Nouvelles Nouvelles*: "Or voy je bien que je suis frict" (XXXIII, 334).

236. *turoit*, reduced conditional of *tuer* (Marchello-Nizia, p. 223).

239. *hochement* 'shaking, nodding' with obscene meaning. See Huguet, *s.v. hocher*: "secouer (dans un sens libre). Ils appointerent avec ce maistre trompette, qui estoit venu un peu devant pour hocher la chambriere."

241. 'I shall be dressed out like a gosling.'

243. *gaigne* from the *Guillebert* is glossed by Huguet "colère," but he suggests a correction to *graigne* without assigning a meaning to the latter.

244. *desvé* (OF *desver*) 'mad.'

254. *bouté a l'acul* is, according to Cotgrave, a hunting term meaning to be thrust, backed into a corner where the animal, sitting on its tail, prepares to defend itself.

255. Imp. *col.* Cf. the proverb cited by Nicot: *Mal est caché, à qui le cul appert*, translated *Si postrema patent, non bene cuncta latent.*

258. Imp. *asseure*.

258. *ra*, from *ravoir* 'to extricate oneself.' Cf. *Les Cent Nouvelles Nouvelles: mais le pis fut qu'elle demoura en chemin, sans se povoir ravoir, ne monter, ne avaler, quelque peine qu'elle y mist* (XL, 80-82).

263. *raine* 'frog.' Cf. the *Roman de Renard: Et il gist en cel fossé mors, Tot estendu con une raine* (*T.-L.*, VIII, 202).

267. *estre a bazac* 'be destroyed, undone.'

272. *encresté* 'proud, stately.' Cf. Rabelais: "Les aultres enfloyent en longueur par le membre qu'on nomme le laboureur de nature, en sorte qu'ilz le avoyent merveilleusement long, grand, gras, gros, vert et *acresté* a la mode antique (II, 1)."

280. *robille* "The clothes, rings, Jewels, and attire of a widow...adjudged unto her upon her renouncement of her deceased husbands estate" (Cotgrave). Extended to a religious, the word meant "Hardes laissées par un religieux à sa mort" (*Dic. Gen.*).

282. *fienter* "to dung, shite, scumber" (Cotgrave).

286. *tout fin plat* 'completely prostrate.'

289. *puteur* "puanteur" according to Huguet, but he cites only this passage.

292. Imp. *p. lavez vous*. The correction was suggested by Philipot, p. 239, as consistent with Normano-Picard phonology.

294. *mis en mue* 'hidden, sequestered,' a hunting expression referring to the placing of a hawk in a cage to molt.

303. *a pourveoir* 'into safe keeping.'

309. *poinctifz comme linotz* 'pert as a linnet.'

311. *custodinos*, literally one who was, in name only, the possessor of an ecclesiastical benefice with the obligation to return it one day to the true holder (Huguet). Its obscene meaning is given by Huguet from this passage alone.

312. *brelicques*?

313. *flicques* 'flich of bacon' (Cotgrave assigns the form to the Picard region for French *fliche*). Philipot, p. 239, interprets the word as "cuisses maigres" as opposed to *jambons* (314).

323. *muguet* "A fond woer, or courter of wenches" (Cotgrave). For *grateurs de pareilz*, see Philipot: "Obscure. Je conjecture: norm. *parei, paroi*: Les muguets grattent la cloison de la chambre de leurs belles pour se faire ouvrir" (p. 240).

332. *brongnes*, which Montaiglon misread as *trongnes*, is a Picard survival of OF *broigne*, here designating neck armor of some sort, hence by metonomy the throat: *lavant leurs brongnes* 'rinsing their throats' (see Philipot, p. 240).

335. *sorir*, which Montaiglon misread as *sotir*, "to drie, or make red (as Herrings) in the smoke" (Cotgrave). The missing verse makes it difficult to understand the expression, but we should doubtless read 'to keep my throat from drying out.' Huguet records this single example of *sotir* with a question mark, hence it should be deleted.

342. A nonsensical Latin outburst: 'Into thy hands, O Lord, unless it not trouble, Lord, the spirit and flesh, I confess to God on high, a crowd of prophets may be able. . .'. This contains several scriptural and liturgical passages: *Pater, in manus tuas commendo spiritum meum*, Christ's last words on the cross (Luke 23: 46, repeating Psalm 30:6); *Confiteor Deo omnipotenti* (from the Ordinary of the Mass). Perhaps this passage was inspired by Rabelais where the enemies of Frere Jean beg for confession before death: *Confiteor! Miserere! In manus!* (I, 26).

350. *sainct Gens*, invoked as a favorite oath, seems unknown. André Tissier, *La farce en France de 1450 à 1550* (Paris, 1967), p. 223, suggests that it is a deformation of *sainct Jehan*, but I propose to identify this saint with Saint Gentien (GENTIANUS) whose cult, along with those of SS. Valery (278) and Firmin (269) invoked in the course of the *Guillebert*, is centered in Amiens, quite near to Meullers. In the left porch of the façade of Amiens cathedral is sculpted the figure of Saint Firmin, who first brought the faith to the Ambiani, surrounded by statues of the first martyrs of the region, and among them Saint Gentien. See Emile Mâle, *L'Art religieux au XIIIe siècle* (Paris, 1910), p. 305.

352. *je varie* 'I am on the verge of' (see Philipot, p. 240).

354. *couronne* 'tonsured head.'

355. *gravonner* "To proke, or dig, with the fingers, into the ground" (Cotgrave), hence 'to torment' (see Philipot, p. 239, who assigns it to the Norman dialect at this period).

356. *tesnier* 'den, lair,' unusual in the masculine but traced by Philipot, p. 240, to Norman French. Its metaphoric sense was doubtless influenced by *testicle*. *pelus* 'hairy.'

359. *ille*, masculine singular tonic pronoun (= *bissac*), but it seems feminine plural at vs 383 (= *les brayes*) which Marchello-Nizia claims to be Northern and Eastern in Middle French. We could perhaps correct to the masculine singular *ce est ille* (383) to agree with *le* (380) and *il* (381), with *sac* (379) as antecedent, especially since *prins* is masculine.

366. *je feray le cas* 'I'll reckon up.'

368. Huguet gives *paistre pelee* in this passage with a question mark.

370. *mis a sac* 'destroyed.'

371. *gibet*, euphemism for the Devil. Cf. *Que gibet, je suis corrigier* from Jehan Jenin (ed. E. Droz, *Le Recueil Trepperel: Les Farces* [Genève, 1961], p. 71).

375. Imp. *rairez vous*, a correction suggested by Philipot, p. 239. *raire* 'shave, shear.'

378. *despoille* 'clothes.'

381. Imp. *Il frere guillebert F*.

393. *eur* 'good fortune.'

395. Imp. *ous*, perhaps a contraction of *ou si*.

404. A proverbial expression. Cf. *Aux grands maux les grands remèdes.*

(Le Roux de Lincy, I, 262).

411. *c'est bien chië* 'it's not important,' a popular expression often found in Rabelais: *c'est bien chië chantë. Beuvons!* (I, 5; see also II, 29, and IV, 8).

421. *gestes?*

429. Imp. *B. a B.*

431. *estuy a couilles* 'codpiece.'

433. *fresaye* 'screech owl,' and figuratively 'a bird of ill omen.'

439. *margout* "gros chat mâle" (Huguet), but only this passage is cited. It is more commonly found in the form *marcou*.

442. Philipot, p. 239, interprets *foutinë* "fouetté, fessé" and attaches it to *fouatines* "verges" found in Norman lexicons. Huguet glosses it "battre" but he cites only this passage.

444. Imp. *huihot*, unlikely since it would be identical with its rhyme word. Philipot, p. 240, supposes, and correctly I think, a misprint for *buihot* (OF *buhot, buihot*), a Northern word for "tuyau, gaine," with obscene meaning (see Tilander, p. 87, *T.-L.*, 1193, and Godefroy, *s. v. buhot*).

445. *huihot* 'cuckold,' specifically Picard and Walloon which Philipot, p. 240, derives from the diminutive of *Wilhelm* (see n. 103 to Jean de Condé's *Les Braies le prestre*).

447. *engë* 'embarrassé.' *Que maudit soit qui m'a engë de ta charongne* (Huguet).

472. This line is doubtless spoken by the *commere*, not the *femme*.

479. *on*, subject pronoun first person plural. *S'on ne sommes mors ou tuës* cited by Marchello-Nizia, p. 176, as a syntactical feature of the North East.

481. Imp. *J. je ne.*

499. *fiens* "Dung, ordure" (Cotgrave).

503. Imp. *m'a. jamais n'y.*

513. *sans plus de plaict* 'without further ado.'

524. "*degrè* in an envoi often refers to the steps of an amphitheatre. This could be a pun spoken as the actors leave the stage by climbing up the steps of the amphitheatre, or it could mean 'in due order of precedence,' i.e. in an orderly manner" (Bowen, *Four Farces*, n. 194 to *l'Obstination des femmes*).

525. The concluding two-part formula, *Adieu* and *prenez en gre*, is described by Bowen, *Caractèristiques*, pp. 63-64, who notes that the two are often combined, as they are here. The failure to mention *dames* or *damoyselles*, as is often the case in the farce, suggests that the *Guillebert* was written for and performed before an all-male audience. This supports Philipot's conclusion that the farce was the product of a group of young, secular clergy at Meullers.

4. Henri Estienne

The *Apologie pour Hérodote* (1566),[1] written by the renaissance scholar Henri Estienne (Stephanus), is a satiric work of ambitious proportions aimed at contemporary French society. One of the recurrent themes of the *Apologie* involves attacks against the abuses of the Catholic clergy, and especially the Franciscans (there are no fewer than twenty-eight anecdotes about unworthy Minorites). In Chapter XXI, entitled *De la Lubricité et Paillardise des Gens d'Eglise* (II, 20-22), Estienne recounts this story, described in the Table (II, 434) as follows:

Un cordelier, sous prétexte de porter les reliques de S. Bernardin à la femme d'un médecin, se couche auprès d'elle: ou ayant laissé ses brayes, les revint querir le lendemain en belle procession.

Item on lit de plusieurs par le conseil desquels les femmes feignoyent estre malades de quelcune des maladies ausquelles leur sexe est subject, à fin que sous couleur de leur apporter les reliques et de leur applicquer, ils eussent moyen de leur applicquer autre chose. Comme sceut bien faire en Sicile un frère mineur à la jeune femme d'un vieil médecin: car elle nommée Agathe ayant descouvert en sa confession à ce moine une partie de ce qu'elle avoit sur le cueur, et principalement le desgoustement qu'elle avoit de son mari, et ayant assez donné à entendre (au moins à un si bon entendeur) qu'elle cercheroit volontiers appétit ailleurs, la conclusion fut prise (avant que luy bailler l'absolution) que le lendemain, sitost que son mari seroit parti pour aller à sa pratique, elle feindroit estre malade d'une suffocation de la matrice (comme de vray ell'y estoit un peu subjecte) et lors ell'invoqueroit l'aide de monsieur S. Bernardin. Ce qui fut faict: de sorte qu'on alla supplier ce gentil frère mineur qu'il luy pleust apporter à cette povre patiente les miraculeuses reliques de monsieur S. Bernardin. Luy, joyeux de ce que sa trame estoit en si bons termes, ne fut paresseux: mais arrivant au lict de la malade, et y trouvant plus de tesmoins qu'il n'estoit besoin, dict qu'il faloit commancer par la saincte confession; lequel mot fut suffisant pour les faire retirer: de sorte qu'avec luy ne demeure que son

---

[1] P. Ristelhuber, *Apologie pour Hérodote: Satire de la société au XVIe siècle par Henri Estienne: Nouvelle édition, faite sur la première et augmentée de remarques,* 2 vols. (Paris, 1879).

compagnon et la chambrière de ladicte patiente. Et alors fut question tant à maistresse qu'à chambrière d'employer le temps à autre chose qu'à confession. Or ainsi qu'ils estoyent bien en train, arrive le povre médecin (ne donnant loisir au porteur de reliques de rechausser ses brayes, mais seulement de sortir du lict): lequel trouvant ces deux beaux pères si près de sa femme, commença à se gratter la teste, n'osant pas dire tout ce qu'il en pensoit: et ce qui rengrégea bien son mal de teste, fut qu'après leur départ, en racoustrant l'oreiller de sa femme, il trouva derrière, les brayes d'un desdicts beaux pères. Mais comme la moralité avoit esté bien jouée, encore sceut-on mieux jouer la farce. Car la femme incontinent prévenant, vint à dire:

—Mon ami, voyant que la relique du glorieux S. Bernardin m'avoit guerie, j'ay prié le beau père qu'il me la laissast, craignant que le mal me reprist.

Ce moine, averti par la chambrière de ceste eschappatoire qu'avoit trouvée sa maistresse, pour achever le jeu de mesme qu'il estoit commancé, retourna querir ces brayes à grand branle et quarrillon de cloches, avec la croix et l'eau béniste, accompagné de tout le couvent, et mesmement du gardien: lequel les ayant desvelopées du beau linge blanc où ceste femme les avoit mises, les fit baiser à toute l'assistance, et au povre mari tout le premier: puis les ayant serrées en un certain tabernacle, s'en retourna avec ce précieux et si miraclifique joyau. Les autres (desquels est Poge) racontent que ce furent les brayes de S. François qui couvrirent le déshonneur du haut de chausse qui avoit esté laissé par le frere mineur.

5. *La Culotte des Cordeliers*

Pierre-Jean-Baptiste Le Grand d'Aussy was a devoted disciple of the great eighteenth-century medievalist La Curne de Sainte-Palaye whose transcriptions of short narrative works from Old French he used for his adaptations into French prose.[1] Le Grand provided his collection with a 109-page preface which, along with rambling remarks regarding the literary situation of medieval France, attempted to justify his labors by claiming for his work the age-old intention of "plaire et instruire" (ii). Although he was considerably advanced over his contemporaries in his appreciation of medieval literature, Le Grand nonetheless felt the need, in eighteenth-century fashion, to apologize for much of "cette écume grossiere d'un tems d'ignorance" (x), and especially when it came to his third category of poetry, the *conte*. Much of what Le Grand read in La Curne's materials and in manuscripts of the Royal Library in Paris shocked and disgusted him: "Les expressions, pires encore, y sont ordinairement d'une grossiéreté qui révolte" (lxxix), but as an honest historian he was constrained to treat them as they were, "puisqu'elles peignent leur siecle" (lxxii), with the exception of the more licentious stories which he either omitted altogether or presented with the objectionable passages excised. "Ce n'est point là dépouiller un Auteur, c'est le mettre en état d'entrer chez les honnêtes gens" (lxxiii). In his version of *Les Braies au cordelier*, the bedroom scene between the wife and the clerc (vss 79-88) must have fallen into the category of eighteenth-century impropriety and, accordingly, Le Grand deleted it from his version of the story. I reproduce below the adaptation of the fabliau as it appears in Vol. II, pp. 66-73, of Le Grand d'Aussy's collection.

---

[1] *Fabliaux ou contes du XIIe et du XIIIe siecle, traduits ou extraits d'après divers manuscrits du tems,* 3 vols. (Paris, 1779), published without the author's name. On the rise of medieval scholarship in the eighteenth century, see the fine study by Lionel Gossman, *Medievalism and the Ideologies of the Enlightenment: The World and Work of La Curne de Sainte-Palaye* (Baltimore, 1968). Le Grand d'Aussy and his collection of fabliaux have been the object of a monograph by G. J. Wilson, *A Medievalist in the Eighteenth Century* (The Hague, 1975).

La Culotte des Cordeliers

Je vais vous conter une plaisante aventure, arrivée à Orléans lorsque j'y étais. Vous pouvez en toute sûreté m'en croire, car je la fais de source, et j'en ai connu le héro.

Une Orléanaise avait pour ami un Clerc. Quand une femme entreprend de jouer ce jeu-là, elle doit être adroite et rusée; il faut qu'elle sache mentir avec hardiesse, qu'elle ait un esprit fertile en expédiens, et surtout ne se déconcerte jamais. Or, telle était au suprême degré notre bourgeoise, et jamais vous n'avez connu plus fine commere. Son époux au contraire, nommé Michel, et Marchand de son métier, était un bon-homme.

Apellé de tems en tems, par son commerce, aux foires ou aux marchés voisins, il eut besoin d'aller à celui de Meun. Un sien cousin, nommé Guillaume, devant y aller aussi, ils convinrent de partir ensemble. Notre époux même promit d'aller le prendre; et en conséquence il chargea sa femme de l'éveiller au point du jour, et se coucha de bonne-heure. Celle-ci, tres-aise de cette absence, comme vous pouvez croire, et resolue d'en profiter, voulut promptement se débarasser de lui. Il était à peine dans son premier somme, qu'elle le réveilla brusquement:

—Eh! vîte, Sire, levez-vous; nous avons trop dormi, vous n'arriverez jamais à tems.

Le bon-homme, quoiqu'il fût encore resté au lit volontiers, et qu'il sentît bien à ses yeux qu'il lui manquait quelques heures, se leva néanmoins promptement, et partit.

Je n'ai pas besoin de vous dire maintenant que le Clerc avait été prévenu du départ; et vous vous doutez bien qu'il était-là aux aguets, pour entrer dès que l'autre serait sorti. Au signal convenu, il se glissa furtivement dans la maison, où dans un instant il reçut plus de caresses et de baisers que le bon Michel peut-être n'en avait reçu pendant tout le tems de son mariage.

. . . .
. . . .

Cependant le mari était arrivé à la porte du cousin. Il frappait à coups redoublés pour le réveiller, et l'appellait à tue-tête, jurant intérieurement après lui d'être obligé de l'attendre.

—Mais vous êtes donc fou, répondit Guillaume par sa fenêtre, de vouloir vous mettre en route à une pareille heure. Est-ce que vous rêvez, dites moi? Comment morbleu, il n'est pas minuit!

—Quoi! il n'est pas minuit! Eh! ma femme m'a dit que nous partions trop tard, et que nous n'arriverions jamais.

—Votre femme s'est moquée de nous, cousin; allez vous recoucher, croyez-moi, et dormez encore quelques heures.

Il s'en revint donc chez lui, et appela pour se faire ouvrir.

—Ciel! c'est mon mari, s'écria la femme; vîte sortez et allez vous cacher quelque part, je trouverai des moyens de vous faire évader.

Le galant fit à la hâte un paquet de ses hardes, et se sauva dans la chambre voisine; mais dans l'obscurité, il ne s'apperçut point qu'il laissait sa culotte. Le mari s'impatientait à la porte, et frappait à tour de bras. Enfin il fit un tel bruit que la domestique, s'étant réveillée, vint lui ouvrir. La femme, quant il entra, fit semblant de dormir; et lui, qui ne voulut point troubler son sommeil, se déshabilla sans bruit et se coucha. Mais alors celle-ci feignant de se réveiller avec effroi, et sautant hors du lit toute nue, se mit à crier comme une forcenée, au secours, au secours! En vain il criait de son côté:

—Rassurez-vous, c'est moi!

—Qui, vous? je ne connais que mon mari, et il est actuellement en campagne. Vous êtes un malheureux; sachez que je suis une honnête femme, et sortez bien vîte, ou j'appelle tous les voisins.

Michel à ce discours ne se sentait pas de joie.

—Oui, reprit-il, tout transporté, oui, vous êtes une brave et loyale femme, je le vois bien; et plus je vous connais, plus je vous aime. Mais, belle amie, vous m'aviez éveillé trop tôt, il n'est pas encore minuit, et je viens me recoucher.

Elle lui répondit avec un ton de douceur charmant:

—Ah! Sire, excusez mon extravagance. J'aurais bien dû reconnaître votre voix, puisque je ne connais qu'elle; mais je ne vous attendais pas, et j'ai été, je vous l'avoue, si troublée de sentir quelqu'un à côté de moi. . . .; doux ami, me le pardonnerez-vous?

A ces mots, elle s'approcha de lui pour l'embrasser. Je ne puis vous dire tout ce que l'innocent lui fit de caresses. Enfin il s'endormit jusqu'à ce que la *Guaîte* en cornant le jour, l'ayant réveillé, il se leva pour partir. Mais obligé de s'habiller à tâtons, il fit un plaisant quiproquo; car il prit, sans s'en appercevoir, la culotte du Clerc, et sortit ainsi.

L'autre, qui par ce départ se trouvait libre de pouvoir aussi se retirer, et qui avait à craindre, s'il attendait plus long-tems, d'être apperçu des voisins, vint prendre congé de la Dame; et après quelques tendres adieux il chercha sa culotte pour partir.

—Que vois-je, s'écria-t-il? Tout est perdu, nous sommes découverts: voilà les braies du Vilain.

La Dame à ces paroles parut d'abord interdite, mais un instant de réflexion lui suffit pour se remettre; et elle assura son ami qu'il pouvait être tranquille sur l'évenement. Seulement elle lui demanda ce qui était à sa ceinture; puis elle alla lui chercher d'autres culottes, l'embrassa tendrement, et le fit sortir.

Quelques momens après, elle se rendit au couvent des Franciscains, et avec un ton de candeur et de naïveté, auquel vous eussiez été pris vous-même, dit au Frere portier, que, mariée depuis plusieurs années, et malgré tout son desir n'ayant pu encore avoir d'enfans, on l'avait assurée que les braies de l'Ordre Séraphique, possédaient, par le don du Ciel, une vertu capable de la faire concevoir, si elles étaient mises, une nuit seulement, à son chevet; en conséquence elle venait prier le Frere, que lui, ou quelqu'un des dignes Peres voulût bien par charité lui en prêter une. Cette demande, malgré l'air de bonnefoi avec lequel elle paraissait faite, était en apparence si ridicule que le Moine crut qu'on voulait se moquer de lui. Cependant, lorsqu'il vit qu'on l'accompagnait de quelqu'argent, il se laissa convaincre, et alla chercher une de ses braies.

Michel pendant ce tems était à Meun où il faisait ses achats. Le marché fini, il s'en vint dîner avec d'autres bourgeois et marchands de sa connaissance; mais le fâcheux de l'aventure ce fut quand il fallut payer, et que Michel, cherchant sa bourse, ne trouva à sa ceinture qu'une écritoire dans laquelle étaient un canif, une plume et le parchemin du Clerc. Il entra dans une colere épouvantable. Cent fois il appella sa femme catin, et retourna tout de suite à Orléans pour se venger.

Dès qu'il fut entré chez lui;

—Femme si prude, dit-il avec des yeux enflammés, vous n'ignorez pas pourquoi je reviens.

Elle ne parut nullement effrayée de ce début, et répondit en riant:

Oh! je m'en doute: mais puisque vous avez fait l'étourderie de les emporter à Meun, vous prendrez la peine, s'il vous plaît, de les reporter aux Cordeliers.

Alors elle lui répéta l'histoire qu'elle avait fabriquée, et son envie d'avoir un enfant, et sa dévotion aux braies de l'Ordre de S. François; en un mot, tout ce qu'elle avait été dire au Frere portier. La premiere idée de Michel fut de se défier de ces mauvaises excuses, qui ne paraissaient que trop clairement suggérées par la nécessité. Il crut faire un coup de maître d'aller à l'instant-même au couvent vérifier le fait. Mais vous devinez ce qui arriva. Le Moine, trompé le premier, avoua qu'une femme de bien, faite de telle et telle maniere, et fort dévote à S. François, et à son saint Ordre, était venue avec foi demander une des braies des bons Peres, et que lui-même, quelqu'indigne qu'il fût, avait prêté les siennes.

—Ah! Frere, s'écria le mari, quel service vous me rendez! sans vous ma femme était morte; je la tuais.

Il s'en retourna chez lui au comble de la joie, fit cent mille excuses à sa moitié des soupçons qu'il avait conçus, et promit de lui faire oublier à force d'attentions et de bons procédés, cette querelle injuste. Parvenue ainsi à maîtriser la confiance de son mari, la Dame jouit long-tems de la liberté que lui aquit cette aventure. Elle alla, vint, sortit, vit qui bon lui sembla; jamais l'imbécile ne conçut une fois seulement l'idée de s'en plaindre.

Bibliography and Abbreviations

Omitted here are those references which, for the most part, are cited only once in the course of this work.

Editions and Modern Adaptations of the Fabliaux

Barbazan—E. Barbazan. *Fabliaux et contes des poëtes françois des XII, XIII, XIV, et XVes siècles, tirés des meilleurs auteurs.* 3 vols., Paris-Amsterdam, 1756.

Bastin-Faral—Edmond Faral et Julia Bastin. *Oeuvres complètes de Rutebeuf.* 2 vols., Paris, 1959-1960.

Hellman-O'Gorman—Robert Hellman and Richard O'Gorman. *Fabliaux.* New York, 1965.

Johnston-Owen—R. C. Johnston and D. D. R. Owen. *Fabliaux.* Oxford, 1965.

Le Grand d'Aussy—Pierre-Jean-Baptiste Le Grand d'Aussy. *Fabliaux ou contes du XIIe et du XIIIe siecle, traduits ou extraits d'après divers manuscrits du tems.* 3 vols., Paris, 1779.

Méon—M. Méon. *Fabliaux et contes des poëtes françois des XI, XII, XIII, XIV, et XVe siècles, tirés des meilleurs auteurs, publiés par Barbazan: Nouvelle édition augmentée et revue sur les manuscrits de la Bibliothèque Impériale.* 4 vols., Paris, 1808.

MR—Anatole de Montaiglon et Gaston Raynaud. *Recueil général et complet des fabliaux des XIIIe et XIVe siècles.* 6 vols., Paris, 1872-1890.

Reid—T. B. W. Reid. *Twelve Fabliaux from MS F. Fr. 19152 of the Bibliothèque Nationale.* Manchester, 1958.

Scott—Nora Scott. *Contes pour rire: Fabliaux des XIIIe et XIVe siècles.* Paris, 1977. (A modern French version of the *Braies*, pp. 90-96).

Other Texts Cited

Ami et Amile—Peter F. Dembowski. *Ami et Amile: Chanson de geste.* Paris, 1969.

Besant—Pierre Ruelle. *Le Besant de Dieu de Guillaume le Clerc de Normandie.* Bruxelles, 1973.

Bliocadran—Lenora D. Wolfgang. *Bliocadran: A Prologue to the Perceval of Chrétien de Troyes.* Tübingen, 1976.

Bowen—Barbara C. Bowen. *Four Farces.* Oxford, 1967.

Chanson de Roland, Bédier—Joseph Bédier. *La Chanson de Roland.* Paris, n.d.

Chanson de Roland, Brault—Gerard J. Brault. *The Song of Roland: An Analytical Edition.* 2 vols., University Park, 1978.

Charroi—Duncan McMillan. *Le Charroi de Nîmes: Chanson de geste du XIIe siècle.* Paris, 1972.

Châtelaine—Gaston Raynaud. *La Chastelaine de Vergi: Poème du XIIIe siècle.* Paris, 1921.

Cleomadès—Albert Henry. *Les Oeuvres d'Adenet le Roi: V Cleomadès.* 2 vols., Bruxelles, 1971.

Cligès—Alexandre Micha. *Les romans de Chrétien de Troyes: Cligès.* Paris, 1965.

Continuations—William Roach. *The Continuations of the Old French Perceval of Chrétien de Troyes.* 4 vols., Philadelphia, 1949-1971.

Courtois—Edmond Faral. *Courtois d'Arras: Jeu du XIIIe siècle.* Paris, 1922.

De amore—E. Trojel. *Andreae Capellani regii Francorum De amore libri tres.* Copenhagen, 1892.

Erec—Mario Roques. *Les romans de Chrétien de Troyes: Erec et Enide.*

Paris, 1952.

Evangiles des domées—Robert Bossuat et Guy Raynaud de Lage. *Les Evangiles des domées.* Paris, 1955.

Huon de Bordeaux—Pierre Ruelle. *Huon de Bordeaux.* Bruxelles, 1960.

Joseph d'Arimathie—Georg Weidner. *Der Prosaroman von Joseph von Arimathia.* Oppeln, 1881.

Lancelot—Mario Roques. *Les romans de Chrétien de Troyes: Le Chevalier de la Charrete.* Paris, 1958.

Lancelot do Lac—Elspeth Kennedy. *Lancelot do Lac: The Non-Cyclic Old French Prose Romance.* 2 vols., Oxford, 1980.

Livres d'Amours—Robert Bossuat. *Li livres d'amours de Drouart la Vache.* Paris, 1926.

Mahomet—Yvan G. Lepage. *Le Roman de Mahomet de Alexandre du Pont (1258).* Paris, 1977.

Marie de France—Alfred Ewert. *Marie de France: Lais.* Oxford, 1952.

Moniage Rainouart—Gérald A. Bertin. *Le Moniage Rainouart I.* Paris, 1973.

Narcisse—Martine Thiry-Stassin et Madeleine Tyssens. *Narcisse: Conte ovidien français du XIIe siècle.* Paris, 1976.

Perceval—William Roach. *Chrétien de Troyes: Le roman de Perceval ou Le Conte du Graal.* Genève-Paris, 1956.

Perlesvaus—William A. Nitze and T. Atkinson Jenkins. *Le Haut Livre du Graal: Perlesvaus.* 2 vols., Chicago, 1932-1937.

Poire—F. Stehlich. *Messire Thibaut: Li Romanz de la Poire.* Halle, 1881.

Respit—Geneviève Hasenohr-Esnos. *Le Respit de la mort par Jean le Fèvre.* Paris, 1969.

Tristan—Renée L. Curtis, *Le roman de Tristan en prose: I.* München, 1963.

Troie—Léopold Constans. *Le roman de Troie par Benoît de Sainte-Maure*, 6 vols., Paris, 1904-1912.

Violette—Douglas Labaree Buffum. *Le roman de la Violette ou de Gerart de Nevers par Gerbert de Montreuil*. Paris, 1928.

Ysopets—Julia Bastin. *Recueil général des Isopets*. 2 vols., Paris, 1929-1930.

Yvain—Mario Roques. *Les romans de Chrétien de Troyes: Le Chevalier au Lion (Yvain)*. Paris, 1960.

Dictionaries, Grammars, Lexicons

Antoine—Gérald Antoine. *La Coordination en français*. 2 vols., Paris, 1958.

Aurembou—Marie-Rose Aurembou. "Quelques problèmes de vocalisme en Ile-de-France, Orléanais, Touraine," in *Actes du XIIIe congrès international de linguistique et philologie romanes,* II (Quebec, 1976), 265-84.

Bartsch—Karl Bartsch. *Chrestomathie de l'ancien français*. Leipzig, 1927.

Burgess—Glyn Burgess. *Contribution à l'étude du vocabulaire précourtois.* Genève, 1970.

Cotgrave—Cotgrave. *A Dictionary of the French and English Tongues.* London, 1611.

Dic. Gen.—Adolphe Hatzfeld, Arsène Darmesteter, et Antoine Thomas. *Dictionnaire général de la langue française du commencement du XVIIe siècle jusqu'à nos jours*. Paris, 1920.

Diekmann—Erwin Diekmann. *Die Substantivbildung mit Suffixen in den Fabliaux*. Tübingen, 1969.

Du Cange—C. D. Du Cange. *Glossarium mediae et infimae latinitatis.* 10 vols., Niort, 1883-1887.

FEW—Walter von Wartburg. *Französisches etymologisches Wörterbuch: Eine Darstellung des galloromanischen Sprachschatzes von Walther von Wartburg.* I—, Bonn-Leipzig-Berlin-Bâle, 1928—.

Foerster-Breuer—Wendelin Foerster und Hermann Breuer. *Wörterbuch zu Kristian von Troyes' sämtlichen Werken.* Halle, 1933 (rept. Halle, 1960).

Fouché, *Phonétique*—Pierre Fouché. *Phonétique historique du français.* 3 vols., Paris, 1969-1970.

Fouché, *Verbe*—Pierre Fouché. *Morphologie historique du français: Le verbe.* Paris, 1967.

Foulet, *Glossaire*—Lucien Foulet. *The Continuations of the Old French Perceval of Chrétien de Troyes Edited by William Roach: Volume III, Pt. 2: Glossary of the First Continuation.* Philadelphia, 1955.

Foulet, *Roland*—*La Chanson de Roland commentée par Joseph Bédier* (with glossary by Lucien Foulet). Paris, 1927.

Foulet, *Syntaxe*—Lucien Foulet. *Petite syntaxe de l'ancien français.* Paris 1930.

Frappier—Jean Frappier. " 'D'amors,' 'par amors'," *Romania* 88 (1967), 433-74.

Gamillscheg, *Syntax*—Ernst Gamillscheg. *Historische französische Syntax.* Tübingen, 1957.

Gamillscheg, *Wörterbuch*—Ernst Gamillscheg. *Etymologisches Wörterbuch der französischen Sprache.* Heidelberg, 1928.

Godefroy—Frédéric Godefroy. *Dictionnaire de l'ancienne langue française.* 10 vols., Paris, 1881-1902.

Gossen, *Grammaire*—Charles T. Gossen. *Grammaire de l'ancien picard.* Paris, 1970.

Gossen, *Skripta*—Carl T. Gossen. *Französische Skriptastudien: Untersuchungen zu den nordfranzösischen Urkundensprachen des Mit-

telalters. Wien, 1967.

Graeme Ritchie—R. L. Graeme Ritchie. *Recherches sur la syntaxe de la conjonction "que" dans l'ancien français.* Paris, 1907.

Harris—Martin Harris. *The Evolution of French Syntax: A Comparative Approach.* London and New York, 1978.

Huguet—Edmond Huguet. *Dictionnaire de la langue française du XVIe siècle.* 10 vols., Paris, 1925-1967.

Imbs—Paul Imbs. *Les Propositions temporelles en ancien français.* Strasbourg, 1956.

Jensen—Frede Jensen. *The Syntax of the Old French Subjunctive.* The Hague and Paris, 1974.

Keller—Hans-Erich Keller. *Etude descriptive sur le vocabulaire de Wace.* Berlin, 1953.

Körting, *Verbums*—Gustav Körting. *Der Formenbau des französischen Verbums in seiner geschichtlichen Entwickelung.* Paderborn, 1893.

Körting, *Nomens*—Gustav Körting. *Der Formenbau des französischen Nomens in seiner geschichtlichen Entwickelung.* Paderborn, 1898.

la Chaussée—François de la Chaussée. *Initiation à la morphologie historique de l'ancien français.* Paris, 1977.

Langlois I—Ernest Langlois. *Le Roman de la Rose par Guillaume de Lorris et Jean de Meun: I Introduction.* Paris, 1914.

Lerch—Eugen Lerch. *Historische französische Syntax.* 3 vols., Leipzig, 1925-1934.

Ménard—Yves Lefèvre. *Manuel du français du moyen âge: 1. Syntaxe de l'ancien français* par Philippe Ménard. Bordeaux, 1973.

Moignet—Gérard Moignet. *Grammaire de l'ancien français.* Paris, 1976.

Nardin—Pierre Nardin. *Lexique comparé des fabliaux de Jean Bedel.*

Paris, 1942.

Nicot—J. Nicot. *Thresor de la langue françoise tant ancienne que moderne.* Paris, 1606.

Nyrop—K. Nyrop. *Grammaire historique de la langue française.* 6 vols., Copenhague, 1914-1930.

Orr—John Orr. *Essais d'étymologie et de philologie françaises.* Paris, 1963.

Pope—Mildred K. Pope. *From Latin to Modern French, with Especial Consideration of Anglo-Norman.* Manchester, 1952.

Sneyders de Vogel—K. Sneyders de Vogel. *Syntaxe historique du français.* La Haye, 1927.

Tilander—Gunnar Tilander. *Lexique du Roman de Renard.* Göteborg, 1924.

T.-L.—Adolf Tobler und E. Lommatzsch. *Altfranzösisches Wörterbuch.* I—, Berlin, 1925—.

Tobler, *Mélanges*—Adolf Tobler. *Mélanges de grammaire française.* Paris, 1905. (Translation by Max Kuttner of volume I of the *VB*.)

Tobler, *VB*—Adolf Tobler. *Vermischte Beiträge zur französischen Grammatik.* 5 vols., Leipzig, 1886-1912.

Tobler, *Versbau*—Adolf Tobler. *Vom französischen Versbau alter und neuer Zeit.* Leipzig, 1921.

Wacker—G. Wacker. *Ueber das Verhältnis von Dialekt und Schriftsprache im Altfranzösischen.* Halle, 1916.

Wagner—Robert-Léon Wagner. *Les Phrases hypothétiques commençant par "si" dans la langue française des origines à la fin du XVIe siècle.* Paris, 1939.

Studies

Bédier—Joseph Bédier. *Les Fabliaux: Etudes de littérature populaire et d'histoire littéraire du moyen âge.* Paris, 1925.

Beyer—Jürgen Beyer. *Schwank und Moral: Untersuchungen zum altfranzösischen Fabliau und verwandten Formen.* Heidelberg, 1969.

Cooke—Thomas D. Cooke. *The Old French and Chaucerian Fabliaux: A Study of Their Comic Climax.* Columbia, Missouri, 1978.

Cooke-Honeycutt—Thomas D. Cooke and Benjamin L. Honeycutt. *The Humor of the Fabliaux: A Collection of Critical Essays.* Columbia, Missouri, 1974.

Curtius—Ernst Robert Curtius. *European Literature and the Latin Middle Ages* (tr. Willard R. Trask). New York, 1953.

Dubuis—Roger Dubuis. *Les Cent Nouvelles Nouvelles et la tradition de la nouvelle en France au moyen âge.* Grenoble, 1973.

Faral—Edmond Faral. *Les Arts poétiques du XIIe et du XIIIe siècle: Recherches et documents sur la technique littéraire du moyen âge.* Paris, 1958.

Freymond—Emil Freymond. "Ueber den reichen Reim bei Afrz. Dichtern," *Zeitschrift für romanische Philologie* 6 (1882), 1-36, 177-215.

Lazar—Moshé Lazar. *Amour courtois et 'fin' amors' dans la littérature du XIIe siècle.* Paris, 1964.

Nykrog—Per Nykrog. *Les Fabliaux: Etude d'histoire littéraire et de stylistique médiévale.* Copenhague, 1957.

Rychner—Jean Rychner. *Contribution à l'étude des fabliaux: Variantes, remaniements, dégradations.* 2 vols., Genève, 1960.